HOME SCHOOLING:
A Better Education For Your Child

by Susanne L. Bain

Third Printing © 2001 by Susanne Bain
Second Printing © 1999 by Susanne Bain
First Printing © 1997 by Susanne Bain

Photography by Sunshine Photography.
Photography copyright held by Susanne L. Bain.

Library of Congress Cataloging-in-Publication Data
Bain, Susanne L.
    Home Schooling: A Better Education for Your Child
    2nd Edition
    Includes Illustrations, Resources, Recommended Reading Lists
    ISBN 0-9675055-0-X $14.95
    1. Homeschooling - United States - Handbooks, Manuals, etc., 2. Parenting
    3. Education 4. Family 5. Self-Actualization

ISBN 0-9675055-0-X

Printed in the United States of America

All products mentioned in this book are trademarks of their respective companies. References to individuals made in text are composites of actual situations, used for example, and not intended to cause harm or denigration of character to anyone, living or deceased. Illustrations and charts are examples and not to be construed as actual occurrence.

How to Order: Single copies may be obtained from Andros Publishing, P. O. Box 12080, Prescott, Arizona 86305-5023; telephone (520) 778-4491, fax (520) 778-4620. e-mail - androsbks@aol.com. Quantity discounts are available. On your letterhead, include information regarding the intended use of the books and the number of books you wish to purchase.

ISBN 0-9675055-0-X
Suggested Retail Price $14.95 U.S.

For Kevin, Sean, Heather, and Tyler.
With Love.

ACKNOWLEDGEMENTS

I would like to thank all of the many wonderful, giving, and insightful people who have patiently listened to us as we ruminated about the effects of public education and developed the skeleton of an idea. To:

John Davis of Liberty Books who spent painstaking hours with us looking through piles of textbooks to find just the right ones. The caring people at Brother to Brother International who work untiringly for free to assure that the world receives those valuable things that someone considers trash, and which is considered of inestimable benefit to others. To the wonderful volunteer families of the Arizona Families for Home Education, and the H.S.L.D.A.

The wonderful people at Sunshine Photography in Glendale Arizona who bless families with remembrances of the best times of their lives and who have brightened ours through knowing them.

The people of *Islands®* and *Sammys®* in Phoenix, and *Macayo®* Scottsdale for patience, kindness and nourishment when we sit too long and talk too loud.

Carol, Stan, Steve, Kris, Steve and Christopher who have inadvertently allowed us to be a part of their family and have offered advice, criticism, friendship. To Matt and Carol Sobut who represent love incarnate.

My Grandmothers, Mabel and Olga, who worked too hard and died too early. Steve Andros, Sr., who spent hours telling me who I was. To Eva and John Schoob, the only other people who knew about the first edition of this book, urged me on with love, and passed away before it came to print. These first generation American immigrants worked and died to build the economy of a young, vibrant country and serve as an inspiring example of accomplishment from the ashes of dislocation.

Steve and Teri, whose competitiveness and drive helped to make me what I am and keep me wondering if I will ever be good enough.

With love to Steve and Jackie Andros who made the sacrifices it took to provide a traditional family at a time when my friends were losing theirs, and who have proved to me that work is its own reward, and that respect is the most difficult thing on earth to earn.

With special love to Sean, who is well on his way to fulfilling a wonderful dream in his good-natured and patient way. To Heather, brilliant and kind, who will soon make her important lifetime decisions and then be on her way to fulfilling the high expectations she has set for herself. To Tyler who has set his sights on the stars and will probably reach them with wit and humor, naively assuming there is no reason why he shouldn't. All of whom have brought me the greatest happiness possible and have shown me the world, helped me to discover the past, magnify the present, and through whose eyes I have rediscovered the universe and keep the now and here in perspective.

And undying love to my husband, Kevin.

Table of Contents

About the Author

Susanne and her husband Kevin live with their three children in Scottsdale, Arizona with three golden retrievers who live on a steady diet of landscape sprinklers and irrigation piping, a growing population of koi, and five cats who lounge around on textbooks and keyboards, fall headfirst into mailing tubes and boxes, and generally make a nuisance of themselves.

-*1*-

MY STYLE

"I should not talk so much about myself if there were anybody else whom I knew as well."
Henry David Thoreau

In talking with other parents of home schooled children, and friends that are contemplating taking the step to home school, I have offered many of the explanations, projects, forms, and procedures I have outlined herein. I spend most of my time working with my children as their teacher, and, as such, I understandably have developed my own brand of relating to others which may seem, at times, stilted, and other times quite repetitive. I have no intention of being patronizing, nor is it my goal to appear to have all of the answers. What is contained herein is a short digest version of what I have done every day for many years. I have related real experiences here which have occurred with our family, our friends, and through experiences and adventures growing together as a family and as a family of teachers and learners. I have learned much from my children.

Each of us must find our own way. I like the way mine is going today , and I liked it last week. That does not mean that the minute this work goes out the door that I will not find something so much better that I want to run out and tell everyone about it. That is the way life is, and certainly so for an idea which is relatively new in my life and in the lives of those I love. I experiment, I change, I accept my mistakes, hopefully mature, and go on.

I have read many books on home schooling, and, oddly, all of the books I have read, with only one exception, have been written by men who are not home schooling teachers. They are the bread

9

winners of a home schooling family. It is possible that they have spent little time actually teaching except in the time that they spend after they return from their primary occupation. Their books describe the work that their wives do with their children. And that is fine. Most of these people personally have never graded a paper written by anybody with less than a graduate degree. This is my primary occupation, and I am proud to say that the work here is my own, with input from my husband, my children, my parents and in-laws, and others around me. Many of the works I have read on home schooling have been written by people with PhD's in Psychology, Education, and Education related fields. While I have attended four years of college, my majors were Accounting, (with a minor in Psychology), with the intention of obtaining a Law degree.

If my explanations seem simplistic (and many of them, I'm sure will), chalk it up to the fact that my audience is generally three children who need to be reminded over and over again how and when to do most everything. That is the nature of children. Generally I approach any subject keeping in mind that I must explain things on several different levels. See, I did it again!

This is the story of how we have come to where we are, which is the successful completion of many years of incredibly joyful, loving, and fulfilling hard work. I accept at this point that I will continue doing this for at least another twelve years unless something drastic happens in my life or the lives of my children. It is not the anticipation of the work which concerns me, but the anticipation that something will happen to change my ability to work with my children.

Home Schooling will be a lot more work than you think it will be. But it will be good positive work, and you will be able to share the rewards of attaining something worthwhile. There will be days when you approach the whole thing with trepidation, knowing that things went wrong yesterday - and then miraculously something unbelievably positive will happen and you will know that you are doing the right thing for your children and for your family. Hopefully good days will begin to outweigh the bad ones.

I have been told that it takes from three months to a year to help a child adjust to the Home Schooling concept. This, I have found to be true. My children fell well within these parameters, but, thank goodness, more toward the three month than the twelve month category.

It is not my intention to belittle, berate or embarrass anyone. My use of vocabulary is how I would talk if I were talking with my best friend honestly and frankly. If something was difficult for me or for the kids, I admit it. If it was easy, I admit that it may or may not be easy or even make sense for someone else. What I hope to present here is more of a guide rather than a textbook, because I am not a textbook writer. I'm a Mom who loves to write novels and help to run a family business. I also teach my children at home. I'd like to share with you how I do it.

-2-

YOUR DECISION

"Decide promptly, but never give any reasons, Your decisions may be right, but your reasons are sure to be wrong. "
Lord Mansfield

Reasons for home schooling are as varied as regional politics, religious beliefs, and social mores. During our first year, we discovered that there are several major reasons for home schooling, but all involve a commitment of time, energy and soul-searching. These reasons may include, but by all means are not limited to

✔ Disagreement with local social mores
✔ A perception of a child's difficulty with class work as presented in public/private institutions
✔ A perception of a child's difficulty with discipline as presented in public/private institutions
✔ A perception that discipline is not what it should be in public institutions
✔ A financial inability to enroll one's child or children in a private school
✔ An inability to locate a nearby private school
✔ A disagreement with non-traditional teaching methods
✔ A disagreement with traditional teaching methods

---and the list grows as we meet new home schoolers and their children. But what is to be remembered first and foremost is that the decision to home school is **your decision as a parent** and **your decision** alone. Utilizing what **you** know about **your child**, your home, your relationship with your spouse, and your understanding of a support system, and a clear understanding of the organizational skills you have, only **you** can make a decision to expend the necessary amount of time and effort you must expend in order to produce the results that you desire on behalf of your child.

For each parent and/or child involved, there is a differing set of responsibilities and perceptions about home schooling. All are as valid or as invalid as the individual's personal expectations. What I know best are the problems and solutions we have found within our home, and therefore, I can best present our experiences.

For seven years, from Kindergarten through sixth grade, we watched as our eldest son foundered in the public school system. We have found that teaching methods, over the years have changed tremendously. My husband and I predate the **open classroom** fad of the 60's, and therefore, probably were the last of the dinosaurs to take advantage of a truly "traditional" classroom atmosphere. To be honest, we did well; even with an average of 35 children per classroom, and a teacher standing before these children with a piece of chalk in her hand for 6 to 7 hours a day. With no computers, and studying with slide rules instead of calculators. In classrooms which discouraged teacher's aids and parent volunteers, we were provided with education which transcended the dubious political atmosphere and social problems emergent during the 1960's.

SAT scores for the 1995 test year rose to *almost* where they were during the *early 1970's*. I find this interesting, because my original theory stands up to this assessment. My theory is this: Academic education during the early 1960s was the best possible example of education that has been produced in the history of our country. The later 1960's, when Open Classrooms and experimental education became faddish among educators, heralded the beginning of a failure of the educational system in our country and the end of the expectation of educational excellence. My personal performance scores were included in the assessment of the early 70's. I took the PSAT in 1972 and scored in the upper 5% cumulative. I took the ACT in 1973 and scored higher. Remember this was a time before pocket calculators had been perfected and DOS had not yet been conceived. Computers were the size of the Pentagon. I know that while I am bright, I am not a genius. My early education was an excellent, step-by-step, broad-based rural education provided by caring teachers in a positive environment which was *uniformly expected* and *assumed* by the parents, teachers and administrators. Our school had a strong PTA with strong attendance, and a School Board which expected its sons and daughters to fare well in the world, and I understand that most of us have.

Comparing notes, we found that discipline on an elementary (K-6) level was maintained by a single principal with the help of one or two secretaries and a school nurse. Maintenance on the average elementary school campus was performed not by seven or eight, but by one highly talented, and respected, individual. It was under these; what teachers would today consider to be untenable circumstances; that we finished our core subject textbooks, learned sportsmanship and found friendship. School was perceived as a refuge and a place of learning. A place of trust, where we and our parents **expected** that our welfare was first and foremost in the minds of the adults around us. We knew nothing of teacher's strikes or personal problems of the adults who cared for us. What mattered to us and to those stable individuals who served our parents was getting on the bus, arriving on time, and participating in a learning experience where we were rewarded for good behavior and positive learning; and **expected** discipline if we created mischief, or, unthinkably, harmed people or property. Disrespect was not tolerated and handled immediately.

Unfortunately, under the parameters created over the past thirty years, nothing of this type of situation seems to exist today. If this does in truth exist somewhere in the United States, write to me. I'd love to share your community with you. We're looking for a place where respect for authority, love, and discipline are maintained, and where police officers do not need to patrol the halls with drug sniffing dogs to protect children from one another; and, frighteningly, from their teachers, administrators or custodians.

Although generally presented as a positive, more loving, more giving, atmosphere, Whole Language curriculum has been accepted as a repository terminology of everything from a representation of award winning teachers dedicated to teaching without the boundaries of desks and with the freedom of removing the children from a classroom environment to lecture in the fields surrounding schools, to an excuse for an enraged, divorced, single parent teacher who refuses to teach above a preschool level. In short, there are wonderful

14

teachers who understand that whole language can be an incredibly useful tool with wide parameters, and there are teachers who fail to understand why they occupy a classroom, other than as a means to collecting a paycheck. Unfortunately, my oldest son experienced five years of non-teaching with unskilled teachers experiencing (very vociferously) varying degrees of personal trauma. It might amaze you what a teacher is willing to confide to 25 seven-year-olds.

From K-6, my son was

☹ Never exposed to a map of the United States, Europe, Asia, Africa, or Australia, and after seven years of education, could not correctly identify even the Antarctic Land Mass.

☹ Never opened a traditional English textbook. Could not identify an Adjective, Adverb, or Participle, let alone nouns or verbs.

☹ Expected to participate in Math-related experiences once a week, leaving him, after sixth grade, at an I.T.B.S. level of 3.2 in Math and Math related functions.

☹ Never exposed to a foreign language.

☹ Never exposed to musical notation, except in connection with piano lessons, which we provided.

☹ Never opened a basal reader, except in first grade, for which I gratefully acknowledge his one and only Traditionally based teacher who is still (bless her soul) bucking the whole language system.

I would hate to list what he was exposed to, however, suffice it to say, he has a tremendous knowledge of the country of Norway, the state of Idaho, and can correctly identify a narwhal. He had spent the past six years vacillating between the Principal's List (with a straight A average) and the Honor Roll (an A average with a B or two thrown in). By the way, all of the students in his classes were either on the Honor Roll or the Principal's List. Not much of an honor.

Needless to say (but I'll say it anyway) we are Traditionalists. We didn't start out that way seven years ago, because we had promised ourselves to keep an open mind and to accept new ideas. But finally, after my son was pelted with a rock the size of my fist and bruised (nobody did it - it dropped from heaven or flew up from who knows where) and later strangled by the same young man who didn't throw the rock; and after we discovered that he had covered three chapters in his Social Studies book during his nine month sixth grade career; and after we found out that he would have one in eight teachers on a seventh grade level with more than a year of experience after earning a bachelor's degree we decided to look into an alternative, such as private schooling or home schooling. We put down a deposit at a local private school, which promised that our children might be accepted, but were at the end of a *four year* waiting list.

We started off our home schooling almost by accident in finding a copy of the sixth level Social Studies book in question at a used book sale. We spent the summer exploring many things we (and he) didn't know about the Eastern Hemisphere. In the meantime, we discovered the our daughter had never been exposed to multiplication or cursive on a second grade level. While, I guess this is to be expected, in a traditional, early 60's Midwestern school, I had learned both my times tables and cursive from my second grade teacher, Mrs. Martin, may she long enjoy her well-earned retirement.

So we started on cursive and times tables, a study of Arizona, and book reports with our second/third grade level daughter; and we started gathering information from a local teaching enrichment store to bring our son up on his math skills. In addition, we began teaching our youngest son to read using the Ph method. This was a dirty word in our school district---we had to remember **not** to say *Phonics* in a public school. Parents in our district derisively commented that the teachers were under the impression that the word phonics started with an "F", and it had become the second "F" word. Now we can say it as much and as often as we wish to----Phonics, **Phonics Phonics!** My second son is now reading because of this Ph word. It happened quickly, quietly and painlessly. Teaching phonics is not difficult and all three of my children learned early the proper spelling of the word.

-*8* -

HOW WE DID IT

"One of the fascinating things about Charles Darwin is that he really does seem to have been one of those men whose careers quite unexpectedly and fortuitously are decided for them by a single stroke of fortune. For twenty-two years nothing much happens, no exceptional abilities are revealed; then suddenly a chance is offered, things can go either this way or that, but luck steps in, or rather a chain of lucky events, and away he soars into the blue never to return..."
Alan Moorehead, *Darwin and the Beagle*

Stepping into home schooling was rather gradual for us. We first contacted the State Department of Education to determine the legality of the whole thing. In Arizona, where we home school, we are expected to file an Affidavit of Intent to Home School within a reasonable period of time after the decision is made for all children over the age of six. In addition, though this portion of the law was repealed in July of 1995, we were required to seek some form of testing for our children over the age of eight years every three years. I would highly recommend regular testing both as a reassurance to the home schooling parent, as well as for record-keeping reference whether compulsory or not. It is nice to know how your children are faring against other home, public, and private school children.

Standardized testing comes in many forms. Check with your county and state governments, as well as your school districts to determine exactly what it is that you are *expected* to do before you start teaching, and what you must do to maintain your right to do it. If you

17

are confused, you may contact the Home Schooling Legal Defense Association (See Appendix) and ascertain specific information pertinent to your state. You may also wish to contact your county super-intendent's office or state board of education. Some states may require that home schoolers register with the local school district instead of the state or county authorities.

Our county, through 1995, provided free I.T.B.S. testing at various sites in our community for home schooled children. I was shocked not only by the number of other home schooled children we encountered; but also struck by their fine behavior, positive attitudes, and the congeniality of the other parents. Things ran smoothly, and extremely organized by the volunteers who gave up their time for four days to sit with our children and monitor the testing.

Remember that if you wish your children to attend college, or if they need to re-enter public or private school, you will need to keep testing records. Remember, also that states may differ in their re-quirements. Depending upon the social tolerance for home schooling in your area, laws will vary, and it will be up to you to contact someone at the Board of Education. I repeat this because it is not only important, but because **nobody will do it for you**. You are pretty much on your own. Again, if you encounter problems, don't understand anything, or are sent a bulletin with legal jargon that is written so that you don't understand it, I would suggest that you contact the nationwide Home School Legal Defense Association, where professionals should be able to give you direction regarding how to proceed.

-4 -

SUPPORT

"Unfortunately, sometimes people don't hear you until you scream."

Stefanie Powers

We discovered that the county we live in has employed a lovely woman who helped to smooth the way for us, listened to our problems, and recommended many solutions, not the least of which was a list of Home School support groups. These groups vary greatly in expectation, structure, and goals.

Home school groups are started by specific individuals for specific reasons which met the needs that those families felt important as they planned for and formed the group for their children. Most of these groups are relatively new, while some have been around for as many as twenty years. Since a specific group might not meet my needs or the needs of my family, moving on to the next group might be necessary. There are lots of groups, and many personality types involved. What I discovered was that, like our family, most families were just searching for companionship, and a certain amount of support from those around them. Therefore, the moniker, 'support group'. Like discovers and clings to like.

Remember to be flexible, and keep in mind that support groups often have rules which will be enforced to the extent that the leadership of the group has power to enforce them. In our growing group of over 200 families, we found that once our group established a board of directors and incorporated, many of the core families thought it necessary to add fees here and there, and make up their own rules and lost its not-for-profit tax status. Be aware that these

19

these things can happen and exercise your voice and opinion if you notice things going awry.

Support groups can offer many advantages to the home school family. They can provide an opportunity to provide play and recreation activities for your your children, as well as an opportunity for friendship for adults and students, or they can provide much more, depending upon the dedication and willingness of the parents and teenagers to volunteer and plan

✔Exchange of ideas, resources and catalogs
✔Exchange of curriculum or individual textbooks
✔Exchange of information regarding legislative changes which affect the home school community in your area.
✔Cooperative learning experiences
✔Standardized testing (Stanford, I.T.B.S., etc.)
✔Theatrical, band, orchestra, and chorus groups with performance opportunities
✔Period studies of history, including reenactments of periods of history such as the Civil or Revolutionary Wars
✔Graduation with cap and gown ceremony
✔Teen groups and activities similar to those sponsored by middle and high schools
✔Dances and formal prom events
✔Newsletters
✔Field Trips and multi-family long distance trips
✔Group discounts to local stores, museums, theaters, recreational parks, and other places of business
✔Reduced price membership to the Home School Legal Defense Association
✔Curriculum Fairs and Conventions
✔Opportunities to pool resources to bring in speakers and specialists to speak to the organization
✔Increased opportunity to network to uncover apprenticeship and internship programs or colleges for older students

-6-

TEXTBOOKS

"A room without books is a body without a soul."
Cicero

Having contacted the County, signed affidavits of intent (which released us from the school district's responsibility), and being advised of support groups, we went in search of text books. We started our search a few weeks early, because eventually we were deluged by catalogs from many and varied groups of individuals. Many groups are interested in the welfare of our children (which is good, but confusing).

Before discovering that our name had been provided to lots of catalog companies, we contacted the schools the children would have otherwise attended, and they were surprisingly helpful in loaning us those textbooks the children would have used in the classroom if they had attended school. In addition the district provided us with a full list of textbooks approved by the local school board, together with information on contacting local representatives of the publishers. Most useful, however, is the district's listing of Essential Skills by Grade Level. While somewhat confusing on the onset, and almost unreadable, we found that the information contained in the Essential Skills manual has been very useful and maintains a necessary slot in our planning when we evaluate the children's progress from month to month.

To summarize, do not panic in the face of not enough information to teach from - at some point you will find yourself over-whelmed with resources. There is so much to choose from that you will probably find yourself with a confusing stack of information and very little clue as how to sort through and pick out what you like. Like a large bakery, everything looks so good, you feel you have to try everything. You are panicking for the wrong reason if you fear you may not be able to locate texts. You might start in the following places:

☺ **Your local library** may have used book sales occasionally. We have two libraries which notify us in with a community newsletter when they are planning on liquidating donated books, and damaged library books. At such a sale, we purchased our son's sixth grade used and discarded Social Studies book for a quarter. We have also obtained foreign language, science, upper level mathematics, poetry and a great deal of literature for pennies on the dollar...some as low as a dime apiece for paperbacks. Some were thrown in for free because we purchased over a certain dollar amount at the sale, and the volunteers were overwhelmed with what they perceived as our generosity to the library. We were, in reality, helping out the Friends of the Library with much needed funds, but our true motive was in filling our home shelves with useful and coveted information that we don't have to travel to chase down. Its hard to find cheap valuable information - its even harder to come by it for free. Its there if you are looking for it, though it may be hard to find.

☺ **Your local school district** or one nearby does something with damaged, worn or out of date textbooks **each year**. It is challenging to find out exactly what is done with these used texts, encyclopedias, and library books. Contact the curriculum resource person at nearby districts to determine whether these valuable used resources are sold to the community in a jumble sale, or whether they are distributed to non-profit organizations (such as home schoolers). Remember 'out of date' doesn't necessarily mean 'useless'. The information may be fresh, and you may be able to obtain relatively new copies with only some cover damage. In such a sale, too, you may be able to find an occasional teacher's manual for a subject you are not sure how to teach. If that district is utilizing a whole language curriculum, traditional textbooks may be ordered and not used below a Junior High School level. We have an incredibly worn copy of an eighth grade level textbook which has obviously been dropped into a mud puddle. But it is the only textbook we could find which covered required studies of the State of Arizona, and my oldest son assures me that it was one of his favorite books----with it, he completed twenty five to thirty pages a day and gained knowledge I'm not sure could be found in an Encyclopedia. Sadly, many school districts take used textbooks such as these to landfills. If you can save a book from that fate, you are doing the earth a favor, as well as your children.

☺ **Book Wholesalers** (for lack of a better term) will redistribute books which they have obtained from the school districts. This is another way that school districts liquidate textbooks, and it is a wonderful idea. For a nominal price, you may be able to locate textbooks and teacher's editions which have been discarded to a warehousing facility. Our local wholesaler, who is a home schooling entrepreneur, sells primarily to private schools, but seems to have a soft spot in his heart for home schoolers. John has come through for us on a few occasions when we were unable to locate books other places, or were panicking when we discovered that we could not find what we were looking for elsewhere. We now consider him to be more of a friend of the family than a supplier. He does a tremendous amount of legwork to fill his warehouse, and because he does the majority of the work himself, he is very familiar with his stock, and is forthcoming with valuable information, suggestions and advice. It would be my wish that all home schoolers (and all parents, for that matter) could have access to such an individual and his resources.

☺ **Teacher's Supply** stores can provide a variety of enrichment books and supplies you may not be able to locate elsewhere, such as lab equipment, exercise books, records, software, flash cards and reading material. We have several in the area, and they have come in very handy to supplement the material in the textbooks we normally use. Books obtained from such a source may be utilized as a primary teaching textbook, but remember, that as a *teacher's resource*, the goal here is to provide primarily consumable reproducibles for in-classroom use. Most of the things sold in these stores are flashy, eye catching, and can be quite expensive. Many of these outlets in our area offer the same discounts to home schoolers as they do to class-room teachers. It can save you money to ask, and most times they will ask in some way or another. I prefer to shop such places while classroom teachers are in the classroom, as it is a little awkward to ask necessary questions while a teacher is listening curiously in the background. Also, during the traditional school day you have the place pretty much to yourself with the exception of other interested parents.

☺ **Home School Correspondence/Planned-Controlled Curriculum.** Before making a decision about anything, you may be wise to consider the merit of the various types of Correspondence Course work provided through many certified, and generally religious oriented groups throughout the country. Generally information about these types of curriculum come in packets of cards once you have registered as a home schooling family, or in the form of catalogs if the school is large enough to have a generous advertising budget. I have heard good things about many different individuals and curriculums involved, and many offer graduation certificates and standardized testing for your children. Such groups are capable of taking as much of the decision making load from you as you wish, and many offer options from weekly mail correspondence, to computer interaction, to monthly, or even yearly interaction as you choose. It is worth looking into if you desire support from educators interested in helping a home schooling parent.

Keep in mind, you must consider that much of the material purchased may not be returnable, so it is wise to seek out other parents who have successfully used the programs for a variety of reasons. For example, your previously public schooled children may find the information presented in a format they are not accustomed to using. They may or may not be able to adjust to the change. Make your investments carefully and remember that costs can add up.

Read the fine print in the catalog and in the brochures, because some correspondence schools must accept and take into account the local educational laws for their state, which may differ, and be more or less stringent than your own. Also, the requirements, time limitations, record keeping, and courses of study may be of a type you disagree with, or just don't feel you can handle up front. For example, one school will not start a student in the middle of a year. A child pulled from a public school in January as a sixth grader may find herself starting sixth grade over again with a correspondence school. Others are very good at diagnostic testing and pinpointing exactly where the child will start in core subjects. Some will offer, in addition, elective work suitable to your child's goals and aspirations. This type of curriculum can be reassuring for a parent requiring a little more support, planning by an outside source, or regular boosts from a person more familiar with the curriculum.

☺ An offshoot of the planned/controlled curriculum type is being offered by several companies offering **Computer Interactive Learning**, in which your child hooks up during a specific time of day to a teaching institute somewhere in the country, which interacts with and feeds lessons to your child to teach, grade work, and offer help. Another way that this can be done is by sending discs back and forth for grading through the mail (which probably won't last much longer with the type of creative electronics available currently and developed daily). I am sure with the advent of the internet that this will shortly become the fastest, easiest way of sending information back and forth from teachers to our children in the future. Keep in mind that this course work is still in the experimental phase. But it is exciting to anticipate that much of what we do manually as of this writing may be handled through the internet within a very short period of time. If nothing else, this may be as good a reason as any to acquaint your children with computers early so that they fall naturally into this type of learning when it becomes nationally available.

☺ **Catalogs** offered by Textbook manufacturers and laboratory supply companies are almost to be expected once you have signed your affidavit through the Department of Education, but if you do not start to receive them, you can start the ball rolling by inquiring through one of the local home school groups. There are lots of companies out there waiting for you to make your decision to spend money. There is also a large group of publishers who won't bother to send you anything unless you call them up to ask them. Generally, the ones you have to call will charge a nominal fee for their catalogs, and the investment may be worth it. In general, you will call with a specific need, having been referred by someone else (perhaps a teacher or other home school parent) and be quite satisfied with what you receive. Again, read the fine print and remember that each catalog represents a company dealing with individual state laws, and run by the rules of its owners. If they choose not to accept returns, or feel comfortable delaying your small order because they are in the process of filling orders for a large school district, they are totally within their rights to do so. It is, however, common courtesy and ethical practice to let the customer know when they can anticipate a delay, back-order, or a possible refusal of return if the customer is not satisfied. We have ordered otherwise unavailable equipment and consumable workbooks through several companies, and have been satisfied with the results. In addition to the hundreds of individuals and companies waiting impatiently to buy your address, we have found that many standard school textbook companies are willing to sell their products one-off with teacher's guides to registered Home Schooling parents. Some won't. You'll have to check around. I guess the best advice here is, again, make your choices wisely. If too many home schoolers attempt to make returns, it may spoil that resource for the rest of us.

☺   **Magazines** are a wonderful source for impromptu 'units' on just about any subject. We subscribe to many wildlife, geographical, historical, ecological, and scientific magazines, and find that the updated articles are of genuine interest to the kids. Once you have ordered a teaching-related magazine, you will (no doubt) receive additional information and offers of discounts. Remember, it is easy to look at the ads, and know that you need every one of them. Of course, you don't but it is tempting to spend lots and lots of money in little dribbles, and deplete the budget that you had planned for other resources or supplies.

Once a month or so, I will find something in a magazine that is of particular interest to one or more of the kids and ask for a report. The kids seem happy to use them in this way, and it almost always leads to his or her reading the entire magazine cover to cover and discovering something interesting they hadn't known before, or that most other people don't know. In addition, this encourages them to look for further information in the encyclopedias and in other resources. They love filling us in on information that we don't know abou: (or that they think we don't know).

☺   **Newspapers** are an excellent source of current, substantive information. We find that our children generally read the paper from cover to cover each day out of curiosity. In conversation, they are able to share what they have learned. More importantly, the information they read becomes an intrinsic part of their learning process. Internet Newspapers are a growing trend, and quite informative, providing a link to other states, cities, and the world. Current information regarding those places studied, or to be studied can greatly enhance the level of interest the children demonstrate both academically and socially.

☺ **Other Home Schooling Families** many times will offer to trade or sell textbooks once they are finished with them. Generally, we are a quite giving bunch, but most, like anyone else, are on strict budgets. I doubt that anyone would wish to make a profit on a home schooling neighbor.

As I mentioned earlier, there are many places to get materials. It is a matter of exploration, personal preference, and budget. Beware. It is very easy to spend vast amounts of money purely from ignorance, insecurity, and uncertainty. I have found that patience is truly necessary (virtuous or not) in purchasing textbooks and materials for home schooling.

It is important to stress that while budgeting for materials, it is my opinion that the most important of all materials are textbooks. In addition, it is of equal importance to leave budgeting room for problems you or your student may encounter keeping in mind that you have an option to change textbooks or coursework as necessary to accommodate the learning style of your student and your personal teaching style. We have five separate Chemistry courses complete with teacher's manuals and lab materials. I remain dissatisfiedwith these courses we have purchased in the past and will continue shopping around until I find the proper materials which suitably teach chemical equations. Once I have done so, these other materials will create a library of valuable reference works. Failure to relate to a given text is quite common and I emphasize that while it is never a waste of money to buy a book, it may be a waste of time sticking with a curriculum with which your child does not relate. Keep looking if things don't work out at first. Eventually you will find the appropriate text or materials.

-6-

COPING WITH HOSTILITY

"Love yourself first and everything else falls into line. You really have to love yourself to get anything done in this world."
Lucille Ball

I guess we are all afraid of something that we don't know anything about. It took three months for us to tell our parents that we were in the process of home schooling, and no matter how well our children are doing, we always have a sense that we are not, in other people's estimation, doing enough for our children.

I grew up in a second generation American family which stressed the importance of education. I know how important education is, and that is why I am Home Schooling. It surprises me that so many people accuse me of allowing my children to 'drop out'. I guess that is what hurts the most, other than the hostility the children experienced from former friends that attended school with them and their parents' thoughtless comments.

Otherwise normal, secure adults say the most surprising things to our children, then turn about and say the opposite to myself and to my husband. The hurtful comments are aimed at the kids, even after we explain what we are doing, how we do it, which textbooks we are using, and how they have fared on their standardized tests. Think about it this way: Who wants to think that they are doing something wrong for their children? They know how their children are doing in school. If these people feel that their children are falling behind a home schooled child, it is easy for them to find fault with what we are doing. Such information might prove threatening even for a well-adjusted parent of a public-school child. Even though the goal of home schooling should never have anything to do with pushing our children ahead of everyone else of the same age, it is unwise to home school for that reason. But these are things that could conceivably, and naturally happen, especially if the home schooled children are using the same textbooks as nearby school districts. The obvious reasons for this are discussed in later chapters, and involve workload, teacher/student ratio, lack of necessity to discipline, general motivation and the number of days and hours available for actual learning.

In most cases, we are sure that the hostility comes from the perception that we perceive others as not to be doing enough for their own children. Home Schooling is not for everyone. For various reasons, my husband and I have found ourselves fortunate enough to be able to work at home much of the time. Home Schooling becomes an extension of the time that we spend with our work. We are comfortable and happy with this. Unfortunately, many families today find themselves pinched financially into needing both parents' income. I guess the only problem I personally have with this is in caring about their children and hoping they are receiving proper attention and care before and after school.

The question of a single parent home schooling a child is pretty much answered through the affidavit which we signed which states that the parents are expected to educate a child. This cannot easily be achieved by a parent solely supporting a family. Check this out in your state and remember that it is important - **you cannot hire someone to home school your child. Teaching must be performed by one or both of the parents.** This is, at least, true in Arizona, and makes perfectly good sense. Remember that tutoring falls into a different category and supplementary teaching and/or enrichment through a private or public school is yet another consideration.

How many baby sitters would be willing to provide a free education above and beyond the work that they perform during the day for minimum wage? This ruling also precludes the possibility of overburdened home day care mothers operating illegal private schools and charging tuition. This, of course, does not preclude a certified classroom teacher from tutoring your child (a totally different endeavor), or seeking enrichment activities for your child, as with music, riding, art, and swimming lessons or sharing teaching responsibilities with another home schooling mom occasionally.

Many of our home schooling friends, and some of the books

I have read recommend sequestering the children at home during 'normal school hours' to avoid criticism. I'm not particularly sure that this is either fair or reasonable. My kids are not doing anything wrong. Quite the contrary, with seven to twelve completed assignments a day, I feel they are just as entitled as any other person to occupy earth outside of our household as long as they and I know they are completing what is expected of them. And they do complete their work. This prevalent attitude may also forward the belief many critics hold that home schoolers are misanthropic child-abusers who hide their children from society and shelter them from reality.

In retrospect, most of the hostility we have encountered has come through rather identifiable forums -

Grandparents always expect parents to do the right thing, and will always question anything their children do as parents. We handled this aspect by firmly telling our parents that our children were being home schooled---that we didn't know how long we were going to continue to Home school---and that as long as the children were performing well on standardized tests **and learning** that we would continue to work with them. This didn't necessarily make for a great holiday season, but it has gotten easier. Some of my friends found the grandparents to be very supportive. My children's Great Grandfather (bless his heart) was the most supportive friend I found during the first year.

School Teachers and Administrators as a group feel threatened by Home schooling parents. They are mistrustful because, having passed four years or more of education, they think of parents as interlopers. What they fail to recognize is that most parents also have completed four or more years of higher education. I doubt that there are enough parents teaching their youngsters to provide a true threat to the NEA, but I know that they, as an organized body, continually strive to do away with our option. Thankfully, there are teachers who admit that once a home-schooled child is returned to more formal education, he is generally more motivated, easier to work with, and more genuinely interested in learning for learning's sake than the average student.

I have witnessed a growing interest in homeschoolers by public school teachers and administrators. We are often viewed as a source of extra income by teachers, and there is a growing movement to incorporate home schooling under their districting umbrellas. Public school teachers can provide a wealth of information for our students, but I am wary of school districts attempting to micro-manage legislation and curriculum regarding home school. According to recent studies, home school need not be regulated since we, as a group, appear to be doing quite well without the oversight and resulting committees, paperwork and regulation.

Friends often have a tendency to play devil's advocate when they perceive that a friend is vacillating on a concept or action. While your children's friends from school may completely accept this unusual lifestyle for your child without thinking that there is anything weird about it, they may, on the other hand, become hostile. Most of these negative feelings probably are a reflection of their parents' or teacher's opinions. Hostility which affronted my daughter came from the classroom teacher she would have had if she not been home schooled for third grade. I find this a little unsettling, since the woman had never met me, but it tells me something about the teacher, since she made pointed comments about my qualifications to her twenty-odd students during the first two days of school which have eventually siphoned back to me and came as a complete surprise. Her ungrounded and frivolous assumption that I was undereducated and unqualified was never questioned because I didn't think I had the time to mess with such narrow-mindedness. We have offset this minor loss of friendship through our support group, and with other neighborhood children. It is possible that she took our decision personally, when in reality our decision had no basis in her qualifications or reputation.

31

-*7*-

SOCIALIZATION

"One can never speak enough of the virtues, the dangers, the power of shared laughter."
Francoise Sagan

It never ceases to amaze me how many people are familiar with this heretofore unknown dictionary entry. Even my mother uses this word in association with home schooling. What many people fail to realize is that each contact with another human being can be built upon as a platform for socialization. Each person who comes to our home to visit becomes a model for our children, and they are interested in each and every one. They stop what they are doing and listen to conversations, then ask intelligent questions. This is fine with us, because we make it a habit of not discussing anything with anyone that our children cannot hear. Granted, the majority of individuals that our children meet as a result are adult. As a stimulus for growth, we have no problem with that because as adults they will no doubt encounter more adult situations than child-child situations. When they enter college, they will not be entering college with six-, ten-, or twelve-year olds, they will be entering with other young adults. In our life, we connect with adults of many ages, and are proud to introduce our children at every opportunity.

We have nieces, nephews, holiday celebrations, social functions, birthday parties, and the support group. In addition, we make it a habit to eat in restaurants, go shopping, take vacations, and go to movies and pizza parlors. There is no shortage of people, and with no shortage of people, there is no shortage of socialization. As quoted by our home-school advisor at the county - Socialization problems with home-schooled children are a myth.

We find that the true socialization problem is with over-socialized children who spend very little time in quiet, well lit spaces with time for introspection, individual creativity, and one-on-one parental/adult attention. Most children under the age of three right now aren't even sure who their parents are because they spend most of their waking hours with a care-giver and many other children. How are they supposed to know what a parent is when they were placed in daycare within the first seven days of birth?

Each of our children studies near a window. Have you noticed that schools today are built without classroom windows? It is a negative commentary on the socialization of the average American citizen that we must imprison our children inside of concrete bunkers in order to safely educate them. At home, we have windows, song birds, dogs, cats, fish, rabbits, quail, and an ever-increasing supply of brine shrimp from a very old experiment. The children are equally as responsible for the pets as they are for doing away with the pests. And they still get their work done. Sometimes with a cat sitting on the open algebra book. Nudging a pet's tail out of the way of a reading assignment is much nicer than being pelted by a rock in a playground or finding an anonymously written obscene note in a backpack.

We know that our children are not involved in gang activity. We know that they do not buy or use illegal drugs. We also know that they will not smoke cigarettes or use alcohol. We know this because we are with them during their days and evenings, and are fulfilling our responsibility to know these things and give correct, succinct information to our children. We also encourage our children to talk about the things that are worrying them, and they tell us the things we want to know because there is no peer pressure convincing them that we are nosy or manipulative. I don't know many other parents who can honestly write these things down and know them to be true. And yet, our family takes them for granted because that is how our lives are structured. By choice.

Susanne L. Bain

-*8* -

PEER PRESSURE

"One is taught by experience to put a premium on those few people who can appreciate you for what you are."
Gail Godwin

We each have a perception of peer pressure, and many of these perceptions are negative, but, to most parents, teachers, and school administrators, necessary. We deal with peer pressure in almost every segment of society, and, when it comes down to it, pressure put on us by our peers generally has something to do with anything that is otherwise meaningless, adds nothing to the good of society, and is short lived.

Every parent gasps when they see the price of 'what the other kids are wearing'. We don't deal with that, because it is not a problem in our home. We have not isolated our children, but we haven't heard anything about their wardrobes for many years. They wear what they want to, and thank goodness what they wear is generally tasteful, clean, neat, and properly covers their bodies. We are not concerned about brand names, because we (and our children) do not believe that it is necessary to be a walking advertisement for a clothing or shoe manufacture for an exorbitant price when there are other comfortable, reasonably priced items for sale by equally as qualified manufacturers who have enough confidence in their products that they know they will be purchased for their intrinsic value rather than peer approval. Much of this type of peer pressure is an exercise in comparing whose parents are easier to manipulate. I am not easily manipulated, and it doesn't matter because my children don't try.

As a rule, my children dress in what they would normally wear to school, wash and brush their hair, brush & floss their teeth, eat breakfast, and make their beds before eight in the morning. My daughter wears dresses, shorts, jeans, pantsuits, and appropriate shoes for each outfit each day. She is fully capable of setting or braiding her hair, combing it back into a barrette, a ponytail, or a bun. My boys are typical boys who come to the table in the morning ready to work, dressed and brushed appropriately. Our children know that we, as self-employed, home based professionals, see to our appearance with the understanding that we do not know what the day will expect us to do, or who will show up unexpectedly at the door. We dress appropriately for occasions anticipated, as do our children.

It has been said that home schoolers are people who refuse to get out of bed to take their children to school. I have found that this is not so. We are not generally a lazy lot. The lifestyle we have is little different than that which we followed while our children were at school. We just put in more hours with our kids in meaningful pursuits.

Our children do not smoke, take illegal drugs, or drink alcohol because there is no pressure on them whatsoever to do so. When there has been in the past, we have made every effort to remove them from that threatening situation. We, as parents, have a right to do so. We do not think we are wrong to insist that they take proper care of their bodies. We accept the responsibility of knowing that if our children do mistreat their bodies while they are in our care, that it is more our fault and neglect than their own. We are here to teach them how to be viable grown-ups. Doing anything else is not living up to our responsibilities, and thereby would provide a negative influence.

Our childrens' participation in activities is solely at our discretion. We will not be bullied or pushed into placing our children somewhere where we do not know the individuals coming in contact with our children. In this way, we can ensure their safety and their psychological and physical well-being. It is our right to do so, and it creates a stable family life for us.

Our children do nothing because it is 'cool' and they do not restrict any of their activities because they are 'uncool'. To worry about 'cool' is to place unreasonable and sometimes, admittedly stupid restrictions on the growth of young minds.

-*9* -

PROVIDING A PLACE TO WORK

"Cleaning your house while your kids are still growing is like shoveling your walk before it stops snowing. "
Phyllis Diller

I have read a theory that children in a home school situation require a separate room set aside for daily activities (a classroom) complete with desks, chalkboard, bulletin boards, storage cubbies, and all the accoutrements of a typical age-appropriate classroom. I disagree.

Although it would be nice to build on a 30'x30' room onto our house and fill it with desks for invisible other students so that we can play school, it is not economically feasible for our family, and it would probably be difficult to explain such an addition to a city or county building department.

Large chalkboards were invented with the intention of presenting information to a large audience. I am teaching only three children. Each of my three children is learning at his/her own level and from his/her own materials. Sometimes it would be nice to have a blackboard, but it is not necessary. Notebook paper, scrap paper, and the back of used office paper works just as nicely. For big diagrams, we keep a supply of poster board.

In explaining difficult concepts, it is best to have a well-lit, pleasant room, which is, first and foremost, quiet. In explaining concepts, it is nice to accept the fact that paper is virtually free. (We recycle scrap paper.) At some point in school, it was explained to my son that in order to conserve paper, he had to scrunch all of his math work onto one page, using columns and abbreviated analysis--i.e., skipping steps. We worked for ten months to convince him that it was worthwhile to use as much paper as possible to come to the correct conclusion. His philosophy of saving the earth by saving paper diminished as he noticed that his work improved, and he was able to concentrate more on the math than the placement of the problems and his work on the paper.

Our children have a desk in each of their bedrooms. They are required to house their computers. The kids choose not to work on their desks, because their computer equipment takes up most of the desktop, and they need lots of room to spread out their books. They do not use the drawers and shelves of their desks for their school work and their equipment because there is, quite frankly, just too much. The desks, though full sized student desks, are just too small, and our children use them much as any public schooled child would use an in-home student desk - to store junk. You may not think this is a good idea, but it still works for us, and maintains a sense of not-school in the place where they sleep and do things other than work.

My oldest son has the best place in the house to work. It is probably the least convenient; but it was chosen because he was an incorrigible chair-tipper in school. He cannot do that with a full-sized, overstuffed sofa. A clever engineer at the college he now attends designed rocking chairs for use as desk chairs in the dorms. Our son can now tip his chair all he wants and never fall over backwards. At home, he also had the most privacy and the quietest place in the house because he is easily distracted and his work required intense concentration. He has easily adjusted to dorm life by finding quiet places to study.

My daughter and youngest son share the breakfast table. This is for a variety of reasons. First of all, we eat all of our meals on the breakfast table, so it is scuffed up and mistreated in the first place, and sees a lot of activity during the day. Also, the fact that the table must be cleared before we eat our lunch encourages our daughter to work through her studies, and challenges her to finish her work between 8:00 a.m. and noon. More than four hours of work, for her, tends to depress her and make her feel she isn't making progress. In addition, from this location, I am more accessible to her because I sit at the opposite end of the table for two and a half hours every morning working with our youngest son.

Quite frankly, the little kids do need quite a bit of on-the spot attention. Providing an uninterrupted block of time for a couple of hours a day for a non-or beginning-reader is probably best. I know no other way of working with a K-2 student. Our youngest can work alone on his math, however, his mind does start to wander, and having our daughter sitting opposite him helps to remind him that somebody is always there paying attention to him. Also, it has taught him to sit still, and not to hum loudly as he works. He doesn't tap his pencil or tip his chair, because everyone who walks by him notices. It is in this way that he is developing self-restraint, ability to work with distractions, and proper work and study habits. By the way, he also polices his sister and brother, and we have thereby eliminated many of the school-learned problems we started out with many months ago.

I have been told that children need to work without distraction. I believe that this is true. That is why the television is not allowed until work is completed. Computer sound must also be at a low enough volume so it cannot be heard throughout the house, even if the children are working on reports or learning software. Many colleges are implementing these same rules with 'quiet hours' between 10 pm and 8 am to provide sleep and study.

The one distraction that I truly believe in, and that is missing in public schools is the opportunity to view the world. We have chosen a rather un-desert-like place in Arizona to live. We cannot see other homes in our neighborhood for the trees, and with multiple trees come many bugs, birds, and reptiles. Each of our children has a splendid view of our yard and adjacent landscaping from their place of learning. They are able to see the clouds drifting by, and they know that no matter what else is happening in their lives, there will be a blue sky, birds, and that life will otherwise go on. No matter how poorly they performed in math today. I believe that it is healthy both physically and psychologically to see the world go by during the day.

I have taken the time to read reports on the effects of poor lighting during winter months on psychological well-being and I advocate the use of light, color, and the perception of the continuity of life to increase attention spans and encourage creativity. Our three dogs play outside of the arcadia door where my daughter and son work, and there is a hummingbird who has made its nest outside of the living room window a few feet from where my oldest son works. We have five cats in the house. There is always something to look at, contemplate, giggle about, and figure out.

Without the effects of fluorescent lighting, our two youngest children do not wear glasses, while my husband, my oldest son, and I share severe vision deficiencies. I truly believe that the difference has come not from a difference in intense study or reading related strain, but rather from the type of lighting used in schools. Fluorescent is cheap lighting, but research is beginning to show that it may lead to vision problems. While we use incandescent lighting, natural light is the primary source used in our home school.

Books are kept in shelves in our family room. We were fortunate enough to find six matching shelving units with doors to hide messy stuff for each of the two bottom shelves. Each of the children have a 36" long shelf to store their books, notebooks, workbooks and teacher's manuals. I've never caught anyone cheating, even though they have access to the teacher's manuals. On the other shelves, we store additional textbooks for other grade levels, as well as reference books and manuals on the higher shelves.

The books come out of the children's shelves in the morning. I prefer that the kids take out all of the books at the same time, stacking them neatly on the table waiting for the work to be done. It gives them a sense of accomplishment as the waiting stack diminishes and the 'done' stack increases. It also helps them to plan their time, and gauge whether or not they will be able to finish by their self-imposed deadline. Once I am finished grading their books, they know it is their responsibility to return their books to their shelf for use the next day. In this way, we maintain a sense of order and sanity in our private lives.

Maintaining a sense of 'home' along with the home school is very important to our family, though others may feel differently. While we can see the schoolbooks after 'school' hours and on weekends, we handle home school much as we do our home office. We prefer to neatly store 'school' and 'business' away while we are enjoying our family time, though our business still takes phone calls at odd hours, and there are many 'school' type questions throughout the days, evenings, and weekends. Reference books and tools are always available when there are questions.

Other families choose to incorporate homeschool into their family lives to the extent that they choose to remodel or add an addition to their home, or they will convert a breakfast area or dining room to a classroom. Whatever works!

-10-

CREATING AN APPROPRIATE PSYCHOLOGICAL ENVIRONMENT

"The only courage that matters is the kind that gets you from one minute to the next."
Mignon McLaughlin

Montessori methods dictate that housework be completed and the room clean before children are ready to work. After work is done, the room is once again tidied before the children leave for the day. This makes sense, and I try to follow these rules as much as possible. It is quite difficult to get anything done in a house that drives you crazy because it looks like a tornado ran through it. Although I am not a neat freak, there are certain things that I do while my children are showering and finishing their breakfasts in the morning. Together, we make sure that the house is in an order to accept visitors before we start work, so that the only mess anyone else might see is a home school disarray that is easily explained.

You don't really want to be mixing your housework with your teaching unless you know how much time you have to devote to a small task and have left yourself an acceptable niche. If you ask too much of yourself as a mother, as the person primarily responsible for the day to day running of the house, and as a teacher, it is easy to feel overwhelmed. A small business can further compound the crisis. With some sort of plan each day (and it doesn't have to be written, just a common sense notion of what you wish to accomplish before you teach) things go smoother and you don't end up tearing your hair out by 3:00 wondering how you got into the predicament in the first place.

Think about the things you say and do while you are with your children. Would you say them or do them while your best friend, or someone you respect immensely is watching or listening? Become aware of the fact that you, as a Home Schooling parent, are not only a parent, but also the major role model in your child's life. For a parent of a child in an established school, we should reasonably expect a teacher to create the proper environment for learning in the classroom. This may or may not be the case, depending upon the qualifications, attitude and experience of the teacher. It may be totally dependent upon the teacher's willingness to present him-or herself as a role model. Like many sports heroes, it has become socially acceptable for these people who have so much interaction with our children to deny their moral and ethical responsibilities to them. This may be one of the reasons why you have either decided to home school or are contemplating doing so. Aside from all these considerations, compare yourself to what you would *properly expect* to see and hear in a classroom situation, and see if, as an outsider you can step away and admire what you see. If not, its not so hard to change or alter the offending behavior, is it?

The lesson here, again, is this: If you wouldn't say or do anything to offend your friends, do you wish to hurt the people you love most by treating them any other way?

After a bad day with your child, sneak in after that child has gone to sleep, stand at the bedroom door, or somewhere away from the child where you can still see his or her face. Now overlay your mental picture of this person as a baby. Depending on his age, this child may look surprisingly like that little bundle you held in your arms after only a few hours of life. This is important to remember, because as we remember ourselves at six or seven or thirteen years old, it is easy to recall just how much we didn't know, and how much our children still need to learn, socially, emotionally and academically.

Remember that this little person is completely dependent on you. Without you, could your child find food, shelter and clothe himself properly? Probably not. But would you have it any other way? Of course not. They are also dependent on you and trust you not to do things that will harm them.

Creating the proper psychological setting for their learning, then, is equally as important as the physical facility that you supply to them. Making sure that they feel they are in a safe environment is paramount. Who can learn in an atmosphere of fear? No one. It has been proven time and time again that children who are constantly afraid do not do well. Some die. Some just fail to thrive in other ways, and might as well be dead, because they cannot be restored. Some are retrievable, but permanently damaged. If you are considering home schooling, none of these descriptions have anything to do with your child, because if you are reading this book, you are inherently interested in the welfare of your child and won't allow this sort of fear to cripple them, or you.

☞ Think about what you say. Think about what comes out of your mouth. Do you sound like your angry mother or father? If you are out of control and not listening to yourself, you may not even know what you've said until after you've said it. You can get control of this facet of your personality, although it takes work. Your kids are worth it! If you fail, take the time later to apologize and admit to your children that you lost control, and feel truly sorry for what you did. It later will become easier to look at your behavior before it happens and re-channel that energy to something useful, or, at least, not dangerous or destructive.

☞ Think about what happens when you become frustrated. In working with your child, you must understand that if you are introducing new material, you will be familiar with what they are doing (of course, you understand it better!), but your child doesn't know the material yet. Let it stew around in your child's head awhile and let it grow. The frustration will turn to pride when you realize that your child understands something that could only have come to them with your help. These little victories can happen each and every day and several times a day with patience and if we ignore our personal frustration and realize that each child his own worries. Try not to think of the learning your child does as an expectation of them. Think of anything your children learn as a miracle to be respected.

☞ Children experience stress, have headaches, and get ulcers. Did you know that? Think about it! As a child, I was told 'children do not get headaches.' Balderdash! I have been having migraines since I can remember, and was treated finally at the age of 26 (I guess at that time my physicians believed it was acceptable for a 26 year old to begin having headaches, but the symptoms have never changed in the past three decades of my life). At the age of nine I had severe stomach ulcers. Adults panic and make a big deal out of it when they have onset of migraines and ulcers. They also receive sympathy. Children suffer with them, just as they suffer quietly with their stress. As parents, we can act as shelters for our children so that we can delay at least a portion of the onset of severe stress for them. If we are responsible enough parents, we can quickly recognize the warning signs and change things for the better before the symptoms become physical.

☞ Children are smart, know what pressures are and react to them, just like the rest of us. That is what makes them interested in learning, why they are ambitious, and why they look to us to tell them they are doing a good job. We have to tell them they are doing a good job every single day. This is particularly important on the days we want to strangle them for making us frustrated.

☞ Children (like cats) can sense when we, as adults, are upset. Even if we are striving to vulcanize our facial expressions and breathe normally, the kids instinctively know when we are controlling ourselves. Walk away for a few minutes then come back. It is a good time to use the bathroom, play a sonata on the piano (loudly if necessary) or take the dog for a walk. Come back and more than likely, you will find that your child is there waiting for you and understands what you were trying to explain perfectly well and has the assignment finished. That is how it works.

☞ What I need to keep me humble is some sort of constant reminder of what it is like to learn. For me, as a classical pianist and harpist, it comes with my music. Even with my schedule as full as it is, it is important for me to spend at least a half hour a day working with my music. Having played the piano for thirty-eight years, it is easy for me to sit down and play songs that I have known for twenty years or so. It is for this reason that I regularly pick up new and consequently more difficult music, switching composers frequently. It is a humbling experience to speak harshly to a child confused with multiplication, then, a few minutes later, pick up a piece by Schumann and realize that is can be equally as confusing for me as an accomplished pianist. Learning the harp, as well, has been challenging, humbling, frustrating, joyful and beneficial. Converting piano music to harp is as challenging to me as interpreting foreign language material to English is for my children. Try learning something new as an adult alongside your children. It is an eye-opener! Take a class, learn to knit, *learn to learn!*

☞ Everyone on earth deserves at least one person to love them unconditionally and under any circumstances. This is not a desire, it is, I believe, an intrinsic need. Again, witness children suffering from failure to thrive in hospitals all over the world. Most recently, we are reading about Russian orphans who cannot function normally. A child can and will die without unconditional love and attention from someone. To your lucky child, that person is and should be you. Even better is to know that there are two people to love and admire him or her in the form of you and your spouse. It is nice to think that my children have at least one person and another to spare to love them even though they may be rude, nasty, incorrigible or downright grumpy. We know and trust that they'll 'come out of it' at some point and become their wonderful selves again. Children without such unconditional love tend to stay rude, nasty, incorrigible and downright grumpy. The prisons are full of them, because, in addition, most of these individuals become dangerous. In creating a psychologically safe, loving environment in which to home school you are also insuring that your children will probably never need to live in a 8x8 cell with bars around them, which is, by the way, not a psychologically safe, loving environment in which to live.

☞ Give your child something for him to love thoroughly, and which is his responsibility to care for. He or she will learn responsibility, even if it is just brine shrimp or a house plant. Cats and dogs require parental commitment, but enjoy love and affection more thoroughly and will mirror your child's affection as long as they are cared for properly and daily.

In a society which emphasizes work ethic and competition, we can and are, as home schoolers, raising competitive, healthy-minded children who will be able to cope with society and its ills simply because of the special grounding they can and do receive from a stable home environment. Constantly under scrutiny, home schoolers are, in general, able to maintain a higher standard for their children. The proof is in their children's competency, high moral standard, and academic success.

-11-

FINDING A PLACE IN YOUR SCHEDULE FOR HOME SCHOOLING

"It's a funny thing, but every now and again she pops through into the sitting-room and sits by the fire for a few minutes. It's as though she was giving herself a treat."
James Herriot, *The Christmas Day Kitten*

During our last year of experience with the public school system, we had two children in school and one at home. We live approximately one quarter mile as the crow flies from the school our children attended, and had to drive approximately two miles to get there because of the way our streets work in our neighborhood. Although the bus stopped near to our house and the morning pickup run was only a few minutes, it would have taken forty five minutes to an hour to get our children back in the afternoon. Consequently, we drove our children to and from school.

Mornings were easy. We would deliver both children to school at 8:00 a.m., then pick up our daughter at 2:30 p.m. and our son at 3:00. This ate up approximately one half hour per delivery and pick up with traffic and waits in line at the school, so we were spending approximately one and one-half hours in the car ferrying children. With a third child entering school the year we decided to home school, we would have had one delivery to one school at 7:30 a.m., and deliveries to the elementary school at 8:00 a.m. and 11:00 a.m. Our first pick up would have been at 2:00 at the elementary school and the second at 2:30 p.m., with our third pick up at 3:30 at the junior high. This required approximately three hours in our car, with traffic, waiting in line at the schools, and waiting for confusion

45

at the schools to clear up enough for our kids to see us through the crowds.

I initially worked with our youngest son for two and a half hours a day. This was solid time, with a little time in between to finish loading the dishwasher, if I needed to and while he was working through math problems or filling in blanks in his Phonics or spelling books. I spent additional time grading work for the two older children and answering questions in between the things that absolutely needed to be done around the house and for our business.

In essence, the time I was given back by not having to tote the kids to and from school is free time that home school gave me. This three hours, I consider a gift that kept me from having to get in my car and fight traffic, and I still had a half hour after I finished working with my youngest son to commit to the other two children before I started eating into what would have otherwise been considered 'my time'. Also, you might notice that my day wasn't chopped into a bunch of little pieces. For example:

✔ I'm almost always at home. This can be good or bad at times. I don't feel I'm tied here with my kids, because I always have the option of turning any outing into a field trip experience. As an example, on a day last year when I felt I would go crazy if I couldn't get out, I combined several exercises. Each of the children took along two steno notebooks. Since this was in September, our city was cluttered with campaign signs. I told the kids to list each different political office on the top of a different sheet of paper as we drove along, then list the candidates and their political parties under each heading of political office, together with any slogans they carried on their various billboards and fliers. What the children came up with were lists not only of political candidates, but also lists of Propositions, which we later discussed when we received the political mailers a few weeks later. Being familiar with the slogans, we have kept track of these politicians, their promises, and the work they have done for the citizens of our community. My children now seem to have a more realistic attitude toward politicians and politics in general, and have a better understanding of the way government works in a democracy. (By the way, these notebooks travelled with us in the car until the elections, and were virtually filled up by election day).

The second notebook went with us into the garden nursery

(which was my original destination). Each of the children was assigned a type of plant (that I needed anyway) based on our water availability and light requirements. One child was given the responsibility of finding sub-tropical, low light, high water plants for an atrium area. Another child was given the charge of discovering full light, low water plants. The third was given medium light, medium water requirement plants. (The three bears of gardening).

Based upon the charts which the nurserymen had been kind enough to display for all of the plants in their nursery (why I like to go there), each of the kids came up with two or three pages of plants that were suitable for the places we needed for. We came home with a van full of plants, three happy children, and a tremendous amount of information to compile into reports on their computers the next day.

The trip to the nursery I had to make anyway turned into two days worth of school work and two days worth of planting, and I still have the lists to go back to when I need to replace a plant that wasn't nearly as suitable as the charts suggested.

✔ Think about how you feel when you have the kids home with you for summer vacation. Home schooling is a little like having the kids home for vacation, but it lasts all the time, and there is a little more work involved. Depending on the age of your child, there may be lots more work, or only an hour or two for you per day. If you go somewhere, you can take the kids with you. They are as portable in the fall, winter, and spring as they were during the summer. The difference is, that everyone you meet will wonder out loud or quietly why you have your kids with you when the rest of the kids are in school. Fortunately, we live in a resort area, and there are always quite a few families around who are on vacation. It is easy to look like tourists in our area.

✔ Your children will learn to appreciate those things you do for your family and for your family business. These daily experiences will benefit you immediately and your child's eventual family, in some ways, to a greater extent than much of the academic learning they will have because they will have practical experience in how to be a responsible adult who fulfills obligations. Combined with a superior academic, *lifestyle*, these children have no choice but to attain success!

Susanne L. Bain

-12 -

WHY YOU ARE QUALIFIED
TO HOME SCHOOL

"Educating our children is the most important thing we, as a nation, will ever do, and we must get it right.

"Education, in every form, must be concerned primarily about results. Home schooling has shown those results. Research shows that children taught at home consistently score higher on national standardized tests of reading, math, and language skills.

"In Texas we view home schooling as something to be respected and protected - respected for the energy andcommitment of parents; protected from the interference of government.

"If I am fortunate to be elected President, I will fight for parents everywhere to have more choice and to be able to play a larger role in the education of their children.

"Although some have called home schooling a 'non-traditional' approach to education, the idea goes way back and is mentioned in Proverbs: "Hear, my son, your father's instruction. And do not forsake your mother's teaching." That's about as traditional as it gets.

"As President, I will work to protect and preserve this noble tradition in America."

This letter from President Bush was written to a home-school mom in Texas, and circulated widely by the Bush Campaign.

When you brought your child home from the hospital, could your child walk? No.

When you brought your child home from the hospital, could your child talk? Of course not.

When you brought your child home from the hospital, could he count, hold a crayon and draw silly pictures, ride a tricycle, buckle his belt, button his shirt, tell a joke, or tie his shoes? Nope.

Are you a teacher? Yes. Because, your child can probably do all these things and more, and it didn't take a certified child teacher to do that on your (and their) behalf.

If you have ever read a book to your child, then obviously you can read. If you can balance your checkbook, you can teach math. If you can go on vacation with your family and follow a map, you can teach geography. Understand? These are all practical things that you do that qualify you singularly to teach your children, because you can explain these things in a way that your child will understand because you have been communicating together for several years already.

One thing that obviously links you with your child is that genetically you are already very close to being a lot like your child. Either that, or you understand the way your spouse thinks. As the doctor told us when we gave birth to our third child - 'the apple doesn't fall far from the tree.' Okay, maybe its not a brilliant or creative thought, but even if there are things that you don't like about yourself or your spouse and your child has this trait, at least you know how to deal with it.

It is important to remember that the rules change once you start bringing your children home to school. For example, its okay to be a nerd (geek, dweeb...you get it) at home, because there is nobody around to call you or your children names. At least in our area, many confused and misled teachers encourage slang derogatory comments directed at bright students. Wonder why? Is it possible that they are jealous of the bright children's accomplishments, or are they, like the other students, propelled and influenced by peer pressure and the pressures of television and advertising?

I read recently in a NEA sponsored teaching magazine's advice column that a teacher was concerned that there always seemed to be a student or two in her class that was 'out of it'. The response from the other teachers? Pull the"out-of-step" parent aside and tell her where to shop for 'in' clothes and tell the child to use slang and stop speaking up with the correct answers in school. No kidding. There are some easily led teachers in the classroom encouraging your children (not mine, anymore) to look stupid, to act stupid, and to hide their intelligence. This may not be true across the board, but it has been true in the schools my children have attended. Yes, my kids were in the wrong place. That's why they're not there anymore.

One of the most frightening questions dealt with by new home schooling parents, or those struggling with the decision is the question of possible failure. I recently read an article published in *Wall Street Journal* in response to a comment made in a former issue which criticized home schoolers for producing future welfare recipients unable to support their families or function in society. The response came from a formerly hypercritical researcher who discovered, after actually checking and comparing records, that there has never been a single case of formerly home schooled child, as an adult, filing for or accepting welfare payments *of any kind*. Indeed, the college entrance rate and SAT scores of the home schooled either stay in line with or surpass those for privately schooled children.

Relax! Most home schooling parents are not college graduates---just incredibly interested parents. Read a Biography of Thomas Edison. **Thomas Edison was home schooled**. He did ok, and his mother was not a cardiovascular surgeon or a certified teacher. **Abraham Lincoln was home schooled,** and, to a certain extent, so was **Albert Einstein.** As a matter of fact, most children, including many spectacular geniuses and inventors, were home schooled prior to 1918. The United States did not start with built-in public *or* private schools. They had to be built and staffed. Before that, children were taught at home. By mom. While dad was out in the field planting food and helping to build the future town where there could eventually be a public school.

If you are reluctant to home school because you know you don't get along with your kids, think again. Do you not get along with your kids, or do you not get along with your kids during the school year? These are two different questions. If you don't get along with your kids while you are teaching them a list of thirty spelling words in the evenings during the school week, this is another question. More than likely, you get along with your kids better during the summer, and on Sundays. We noticed that too. There is an explanation for this that you are probably not seeing if these are concerns that are keeping you from thinking clearly. If you're not sleeping because you're worried about your kids, you're not thinking very clearly.

Think about it this way:

☹ During the school week you see your kids when they wake up in the morning. Everyone is rushed, and concerned that they are going to be late for work, school, etc. Right? It is not a good time for the family, because nobody has time to be nice, just time to be rushed. That is understandable, and nobody seems to have good mornings really often if they are rushed and confusing.

☺ If you are home schooling, you will not be late for work, because your work is home with your kids, and your kids won't be late for school, because you are the teacher and you decide when they are suppose to be ready for work.

☹ During the school day, children get tired because they have to go out on the playground at recess and get hot (or cold), they deal all day with people they don't know very well (or they know too well) and someone they don't know very well is always telling them what to do. So, when they come home to you they are tired, grumpy and probably hungry because they don't want to tell you that they didn't eat for one reason or another.

☺ If you are home schooling, your children deal with you and whomever else you choose to let them deal with (or whomever they choose to deal with). They take orders from someone they know (you), and if they don't eat their lunch you will know it and either make them eat it anyway, or find snacks for them (which they couldn't have in the classroom without getting in trouble, especially a healthy thing like an apple or an orange, because they are messy).

☹ Teachers are notorious, now, for not teaching Spelling and Vocabulary, because its not fun, it takes time, and it is, quite frankly, an effort to grade spelling books because the box they have to take them home in is heavy, and generally grading involves four pages per student per week in addition to a test usually graded by an assistant or another parent. Yes, its daunting and time consuming. So, many have decided that since they know parents want to be involved in their children's education, they can turn this job over to parents. But they don't play fair. First of all, starting on a second grade level, they generally assign about thirty to forty words per student, plus three to five sentences that have to be repeated verbatim on the test. (This, at least, is what both my son and my daughter encountered starting with second grade). In many cases, the words have no phonetic tie, and must be memorized individually. Ten of these words are usually above grade level, and referred to as the 'Gifted List' or some other such nonsense which is intended to coerce parents into making their kids stretch a little harder so they can be proud of them, and later makes the teacher feel good about herself because he or she is such a good teacher. The three or four sentences are their excuse for not teaching English Grammar or Punctuation. The self-generated list alleviates the eventuality of grading workbook pages. Generating practice from scratch becomes the parents' job.

Teachers send these things home on Mondays, expecting that the children will take a test on Friday---*with no in-class instruction.* Parents are then required to spend every waking hour while their child is at home trying to get their reticent child to memorize this laundry list so they can parrot it back on Friday. Hence, the feeling that children and parents battle through the school week, but seem to get along on weekends. I hated Mondays because I knew this ordeal would start all over again. I always wondered what it would be like dealing with this for three children instead of just two, because as soon as I got the laundry lists on Monday, I'd sit down and start making worksheets for my kids so that they would do anything besides parrot them back wrong verbally three hundred times over a period of the next four days.

But, again, the system was not playing fair, because by the time the kids get home from school, they have spent seven hours working (and coping) and don't want to work anymore! Would you? In addition, most parents work 8 hours a day and commute two hours a day. No wonder most parents I know are having screaming fits every night with their kids once they start having Spelling words, and math, and social studies; not to mention *soccer*!!

Real problems start when the kids have homework in addition to the Spelling words because evenings are already filled with work. Even if you don't physically stand by while your child is completing homework, there is still the stress of making sure that it is done and ready by the next morning. Where is your spare time when you are instructing your children between 3:00 and 9:00 in the afternoon and evening? Six hours a night, five days a week, eight months out of the year is a high price to pay for a public school education! What you are truly dealing with here is home schooling under the absolute worst circumstances!

☺   If you are home schooling, you start at 8:00 in the morning with a child who has been asleep all night, and who hasn't hurried through breakfast to catch a bus or meet a school bell. Spelling is not a problem in our house, because practice pages we use create reasonable repetitions of usage, and we supplement in an intelligent way every second day with our five repetitions.   Words in these prepared curriculums are generated in a developmentally reasonable order, and with a discernable cohesion.   If words are spelled wrong in the workbook, they have five extra repetitions.   There is no screaming, fighting or name calling, and nobody stomps off. Not because my kids are any different from yours, or because I am any different from you. There is no negative emotion involved in teaching this or any other subject because we approach teaching and learning from a common sense approach.   In addition, my children are not exhausted from being in school before I get to them.

My son's best friend is fond of saying "Every day can't be Sunday." In my house it is, because I get along with my children every day of the week.   I'm not battling peer pressure, teacher pressure, bus pressure or arbitrary deadline pressure. I know when to stop, and *so can you* if you pay attention to your child's needs as well as your own. The upshot is that I have my evenings and weekends free and so do my kids. Because of this reasonable, calm approach, the student comes away from twelfth grade curriculum prepared for college because there is no emotion - just well-adjusted, self-motivated, well organized study.

-18-

HOW TO COPE ON DAYS WHEN YOU DON'T WISH TO TEACH OR CAN'T TEACH

"When you're an orthodox worrier, some days are worse than others."
Erma Bombeck

When I first started home schooling and attended my first support meeting, the best advice I got was from a young, quiet mother who had been home schooling for about eighteen months at the time. The most important advice was:

Never plan on teaching more than four days a week.

I don't. I mean, I don't plan on it. If it happens, I feel that my children and I have been given a gift, because they are completing about a week and a half worth of public school education in the five days they have fulfilled, and I feel good about that. If I teach four days a week, I still feel good about it, because we don't stop in the summer, and I know that they will still be doing more than they would have in a classroom.

But that doesn't mean they don't learn on the days I am sick, have too much work to do with the Architectural practice, am meeting a writing deadline, fed up with life, or taking a sick animal to the vet. This is what I like to think of as time when my *children are learning to learn on their own.*

It is at these times when I put something creative in front of my kids and stand back (or go hide). It is at these times when I start giving my kids choices so that they will leave me alone and pursue something that will probably be more meaningful than any textbook learning. While giving my kids a basic core education, I can also give them mini lessons in life, and it is a way I can feel good about being human, needed otherwise, or just out of it. For example, on these days, you can assign just about anything for them to do, or better yet, you can give them a choice, or checklist of things to do. , These things might include:

For **Social Studies**
+ Make an alphabetical list of the states, postal abbreviations and capitals
+ Fill out a map of the United States, capitals and main water routes, or have them fill in major Federal Highways and railroad tracks.
+ Fill out a map of the world, with the names of the continents and major bodies of water.
+ Fill out a map of any continent (North America, South America, Asia, Africa---Australia and Antarctica would be a little easy, don't you think????) including capitals.
+ Make a list of democracies.
+ Make a list of monarchies.
+ Chart routes of a chosen explorer (Columbus, Magellan, Captain Cook, etc.) and write a brief summary of their lives and/or journeys.
+ Chart the route of Kon Tiki.
+ Chart the migration of a favorite animal (whales, birds, elk, antelope, etc.)
+ Make an annotated diagram of a four masted schooner, the White House, a Space Shuttle, the Mayflower, the Pacific Islands, a volcano, the bottom of the ocean, a tipi, hogan, Native American burial mound or kiva, or an Egyptian Pyramid, a tree, a blade of grass, or a dog.
+ Copy the Bill of Rights or the Declaration of Independence.
+ List the Presidents in order, and the dates of their inaugurations.
+ Take a blank map of North America and place names of Native American Tribes and possible trade routes. Have your child chart trade routes that might have made it possible for an

Early American Grasslands tribe to have been in the possession of a seashell from the Pacific coast.
✦ Plot the San Andreas Fault.
✦ Name all the mountains in the United States in excess of 14,000 feet.

Science Projects that only take one day:
❋ Start a rock collection w/pebbles from your area, and attempt to identify them using a guide book, or, contact an adult collector, borrow or buy small fragments that can be easily identified and classified. Or, at a teaching supply store (on a good day), you can purchase small rock collections with the rocks in a bag which come with a sorting tray and a b o o k. Each rock can be identified by a picture and description in the book. It is your child's responsibility to sort the rocks into the tray, glue them down and label.
❋ If you have no objection to the concept, trace the evolution of a favorite animal , such as a dog or cat from its prehistoric origins to the present day form.
❋ Utilizing an illustrated book of common houseplants, have your child list each plant you own by common and scientific name.
❋ For an older student - plot the orbit of one of the inner planets (or the moon around the earth), utilizing knowledge of the opposing forces of gravity of the sun and the surrounding planets. This may take several large sheets of paper, a compass, calculator and a good Physics textbook. This was a project I completed for extra credit in high school, and I was proud and exhausted when I finished (admittedly it took me more than a day, since I did all the mathematics on a slide-rule, without a calculator or a computer ---remember they weren't around then!).
❋ Give your child a stack of Science magazines, and have him pick out a subject of interest. Ask him to write a report utilizing the magazine and two other sources - only one of them being an encyclopedia. Specify the number of pages, so that you don't end up with a paragraph at the end of the day.
❋ Build a simple wave tank with a peanut butter jar, colored water and cooking oil.

❋ Build a simple solar still, using plastic wrap, a rock, and a shovel.

❋ Build a fire extinguisher with a peanut butter jar filled with baking soda dissolved in water and a smaller jar filled with vinegar to spill after the lid is on. The lid must have a small hole in it. Have your kids do this one outside.

❋ Grow plants from seeds in small containers in groups. Grow one group in indirect sunlight, or as directed on the package. Grow another group in incorrect sunlight with a correct amount of water. Grow the last group with very little water in the correct amount of sunlight. This will take a few hours to set up properly, if you have the child prepare a chart to keep track of the differences in the rates of growth over a few weeks.

❋ Buy some plant or garden vegetable seeds, and a bag of mulch and keep them around, so that on a nice day, the kids can plant a garden for you and you can do something else.

Your kids may enjoy doing **English** Projects:

✎ Diagram the parts of speech for the Pledge of Allegiance. Most encyclopedias and most English Grammar books have articles about Diagramming. If they don't wish to diagram, have students draw different shapes around nouns, verbs, adjectives, adverbs, participles. (a circle around a noun, a square around a verb, a star around an adjective, etc.)

✎ Use the Pledge of Allegiance for spelling and vocabulary practice. Have the children spell properly and define each meaningful word in the Pledge.

✎ Have the child properly spell and organize in alphabetical order the names of the presidents.

✎ Copy an Amendment to the Constitution or an entry of the Bill of Rights, or re-write either in language that is more understandable today.

✎ Have your child make a rebus story using your box of stickers. Or, you can choose fifteen or twenty stickers, and ask your child to make a rebus story using the ones you have chosen.

✎ Have your child write a story for a younger child and illustrate it.

Or, a **Reading** project can be assigned, such as:
- ❀ Read and do a book report on a classic.
- ❀ Read and do a book report on a comic book.
- ❀ Find an article in a magazine and have the child draw an illustration showing the oddest thing they found out in the article. (In an exercise like this, we discovered that scientists have discovered a strange creature called an Ice Borer in Antarctica that burrows through the ice under penguins and devours them, kind of like an Antarctic piranha....Well, the kids thought it was interesting, and it just happened to be in an April Edition!?)
- ❀ Have the child rewrite the end of a classic the way he wishes the ending to be.

Or **Math:**
- ⇒ Have your child copy his favorite recipe, cut the ingredients so that the recipe would serve two instead of four (or whatever), increase it for five, seven, eleven, or three or four odd numbered groups of people, and for a group of twenty five. Have him make a chart to show the different quantities needed. An older child may attempt to make the recipe for exactly the number of people you will have for lunch that day. (Be prepared to supervise your young chef).
- ⇒ Have the children play chess or checkers, or, better yet, have them teach the game to someone else.
- ⇒ Give the child a set of dice, a large piece of posterboard, and some game pieces, and have him invent his own board game. (You would be surprised.)
- ⇒ Give the child two dice. Give him a piece of notebook paper and a piece of graph paper. Have him throw the dice 100 times, record the number of times each number comes up, then graph the results. At some later point in time, have him repeat the experiment, and compare the results. It may amaze you how close the results are.
- ⇒ Hand your child a jumprope and send him outside to jump to a hundred counting by 1's, 2's, 3's, 4's, 5's, 6's, 7's, 8's, and 9's. See how long it takes for your child to return in to tell you that three doesn't go into 100 evenly.
- ⇒ Watch television and count the number of times the word *like*

is used inappropriately per hour. This is upper level math.

or **Handwriting**

✍ Have your child copy the alphabet in calligraphy. At some point, you can have that same child copy his or her favorite poem using a calligraphy pen and a fine piece of paper. It makes a nice gift for grandma, or something you can be proud of.

or **Art**

❦ Keep a good quality Drawing Tablet around the house for each child. First, have them sit in front of a mirror and draw a self-portrait. It might surprise you, and will probably end up being something you will cherish later.

❦ Tell your child to draw his or her most favorite thing in the house.

❦ Tell your child to draw a favorite/least favorite food.

❦ Have your child draw his favorite toy with them next to it.

❦ Have your child draw himself inside of a matchbox car.

❦ Have your child draw your house, your yard, their grandparents, your car, your cat, the dog, or a horse.

or----

◻ Have your child watch tv and count commercials (this can also be done with magazine ads, depending upon the type of magazines you have to choose from in your house). Have them devise a chart which identifies types of commercial by name of company, product offered, whether it is a need or want, and the type of advertising tactic used (subliminal, sex, humor, violence, ...). Record the number of repetitions of the same commercial during a given two hour segment on the same channel, and whether or not the commercial is truncated in some way to create a second or third commercial. Some commercials are split during breaks. Some advertisers run two or more commercials for the same product/outlet on the same channel). The kids will have to think fast, and if you have more than one child doing the exercise, one can use a stop watch or a watch with a second hand to record the length of each commercial. After the two hours is over, the children should either discuss, or write some sort of a report answering questions such as:

✐Why the company would choose to advertise on this station at this time?

✐How are the commercials related to the target audience?

✐Identify the target audience.

✐What age group do the commercials appeal to?

✐Are the commercials fair? Are the claims puffed, exaggerated or totally true? Does the advertiser lie outright, or is there an acceptable grain of truth in the claims?

✐Do advertisers seem respectful of the intelligence of their audience, or do they make assumptions that anyone who is watching may be of lesser intelligence or age than a person who would choose not to watch during that time frame?

✐After completing the assignment, ask your child(ren) whether they understand why advertising is necessary.

☺Remember, it is *no fair* using a PBS channel!

◻ As an alternative to the last listed assignment, have your children research the history of Public Television, and the History of the Corporation for Public Broadcasting.

◻ Ask your child to research where the funding for HBO, SHOWTIME, DISNEY, and other channels with no advertisers comes from. They may have never thought about it.

There is a good chance that your child would rather do anything than sit around watching television as long as they have some direction. Taking a sketch tablet into the woods is a lot more fun than sitting around the house watching mom work; and much more stimulating than waiting for the paint to peel. Give your child a chance to choose from a reasonable list of things that they can possibly do with their time. Treat this work as an assignment. They may never suspect that you are having a rotten day and don't want to bother being a teacher for a few hours. Once they have had an opportunity to teach themselves, they may look forward to your 'off' days, and make them easier on you than you might anticipate. The teachers in your local school have in-service days, sabbaticals, frequent holidays, and sick pay, in addition to vacation pay. Remember, too, that their year is only eight months long. (Think about it---two weeks in winter, two days at Thanksgiving, a week for spring break, ...)

-14-

GETTING THE WORK DONE

"All machines that use mechanical parts are built with the same single aim: to ensure that exactly the right amount of force produces just the right amount of movement precisely where it is needed."
David Macaulay, *The Way Things Work*

I make it a point never to use my spare time while my youngest is completing a written assignment to grade the work of the other two. There are too many interruptions and it causes a certain amount of frustration and tends to make me a grumpy person. Anyone trying to do too many things simultaneously can become grumpy. Try chewing gum, playing hoola-hoop, skipping rope, and answering the phone all at the same time. It doesn't work and it makes you crabby if all these things are expected simultaneously. Even if these expectations are unrealistic and self-imposed.

After I have finished working with the youngest, graded his work, and he has put his books away, I grade my daughter's work. By the time I get to the end of my grading with her, she has usually completed her work. My youngest son, in the meantime, is working through a computer-aided reading or math program, or watching (presumably) an uplifting PBS presentation. Quietly. In another room. If I find difficulties with my daughter's work, she is now alone with me at the table, and I can help her work through things she doesn't understand. Since she is concentrating on many new concepts, it is easy to put books, charts and notebooks in front of her and scribble and talk quietly without disturbing anyone else.

All three of our children are aware that they can stop what they are doing at any time and find an adult (usually me) and ask about a concept they are not sure of. Unfortunately, nobody likes to be criticized, so it is best to use tact if the kids 'just don't get it.' In that case, it really is necessary to repeat the assignment. To my children, at least, this is a big deal, because they realize that if they don't do their corrections they will not be going on the next day until they have their corrections done, and that will delay their free time. Most concepts in Textbooks are broken down into small enough bits that five to ten minutes of explanation can take care of it. In some cases, though, you may have to go in search of other books.

Using assignment sheets as we do (See Chapter 21) I am preparing assignments for the next day for each child as I grade each individual assignment. While I am grading today's math, I am noticing if there is a problem which must be corrected before the child muffs his way through the next day's assignment and compounds the problem. In this way, I am in touch with each subject and each child.

We can and do forego much of the frustration children may have in traditional school if the teacher doesn't have the time or energy to address and resolve small crises. My work today will create the children's work tomorrow, so my children won't watch Disney's version of *Alice in Wonderland* during school hours because the teacher was called away to the district office, or her child is ill (and believe me, they did; sometimes crammed 60 to a classroom). By virtue of the fact that there is an itemized list of things to do, the children are therefore motivated both by curiosity, by increased skills, and by interest in later free time to correct, ask questions, and complete assignments as a routine without argument because the directions are very clear and they understand what is expected of them. They also understand the consequences if the work is not completed correctly---either more work tomorrow, or the delay of free time either today or tomorrow.

-15-

DEALING WITH CONCEPTUAL PROBLEMS

"Kind words can be short and easy to speak, but their echoes are truly endless."
Mother Teresa

It is best not to get into the habit of running out and buying a new book every time a concept does not come easily to one of the kids. This happens frequently. If you care a great deal about your child, not 'getting through' will bother you.

We have found that the best option in this instance is a plan I've adopted until I figure out something better to do (in the meantime, it seems to work and keep things calm)

✔Sit down and explain the topic to the child when you discover the problem. Use diagrams, charts, maps, or graphs if necessary. Explain until you run out of ideas, but no more than your child (and you) can tolerate; probably no more on one subject than about 20 to 30 minutes of concentrated effort. Keep a grip on yourself and recognize that this is probably the first time that your child has ever come in contact with this information or concept. Don't be angry if your child does not accept the concept easily. Remember how difficult it was to learn how to use your computer programs and imagine spending several hours each day with new concepts. It can be quite daunting.

✔Sleep on it. Let your child digest the information. In the meantime, your subconscious will probably be formulating an

63

alternative way of explaining it tomorrow if you need to.

✔Have the child repeat the assignment. If you originally assigned the 'even' numbered problems, have your student repeat those problems, including the ones you used as examples the day before, using the notes you showed her. No. This is not cheating. Its learning. At this time, you may wish to consult with additional resources (other books of a similar nature) if available.

✔Hang around while your child is repeating the assignment, and look over her shoulder occasionally. Do not allow your child to repeat an entire assignment incorrectly a second or a third time. If there still seems to be a glaring problem, stop immediately and try to re-explain the concept. Remember that your child may think differently than you do. An explanation of the concept that you may not totally have faith in may spark understanding in your child. After you have given it another try, let the child move on to other work. A child's mind will continue to work on a concept it worries about.

✔Sleep on it again. Your mind may figure out something you missed, or light bulb may go on in your child's head.

✔Again, try the assignment. You might shift over to the 'odd' problems, if you feel the child may have memorized the 'even' answers. If you notice that the problem is still there, consult with your spouse (as you already may have) There may be an explanation you are missing and two minds are always better than one in problem solving.

✔At this point, you may wish to look through some of your catalogs to find elementary enrichment materials, or visit your local teaching supply store. Allow your child to continue on in the book in question as long as the concept that has slipped by doesn't have bearing on future assignments. If it does, you will be guilty of leaving your child behind academically and defeating your purpose. This could have been one of the pitfalls of the schools which encouraged you to home school in the first place.

We have found, with our children, that the following concepts have proposed these types of problems (they can be found in every subject, but these are examples of simple concepts that easily elude a young mind) I have found excellent additional work for my children in each of these problem areas

> fractions
> telling time
> multiplication/division

> money
> reading comprehension
> map reading
> algebraics
> geometric shapes
> measurement of area
> three or four digit numeric addition and subtraction
> > with carries and borrows
> chemical equations
> scientific classification
> outlining

I have found that the best way to tackle relatively simple mathematical operations concepts is through practice each day. I provide all three of my children with simple one or two-digit problems daily with a publication entitled *Mad Minutes*. While this is probably one of the single most expensive investments I have made ($30.00 per copy), each book provides approximately one year of practice in addition, multiplication, subtraction, division, fractional reduction and percentages and provides a vehicle to promote memorization of essential facts. In addition, Houghton Mifflin also publishes small format practice manuals on each grade level. These handy little books establish practice in word problems and already learned concepts ten to twelve problems at a time and cover approximately eight months of worksheets which take approximately three to five minutes a day to complete at a very nominal cost per book.

The *Saxon Mathematics* system provides this additional math practice without the need for additional enrichment books, however, the practice lessons which go along with the topics taught per day are relatively limited, and emphasis is made on review rather than introduction and practice of new concepts. This concept is great for kids who look at the long lists of math problems in a traditional textbook and panic. Pages are laid out in black ink, with no color separations, but there is a variety of word problems with interesting and curiously witty story lines.

Keeping an eye out for bargains on subject texts which could potentially cause problems later might be advantageous if you intend to continue to home school, raise children who will be educated in any manner, and wish to provide additional help if and when it is needed. Admittedly, teaching core subjects involves stepping off into subject areas which may or may not have caused anxiety for you as a child in school. Keep in mind that you are no longer the student, but the teacher. It is best not to pass along your anxieties until you have successfully taught the course work. It will make a funny story later, but telling your children that you never did well in Math (English, Science, Social Studies or "Underwater Basket Weaving") and that they probably don't need to either will not help them unless you wish to create a similar anxiety for them. Create an atmosphere of confidence, pay attention to the text, and you will do fine. Remember, most textbooks are written at or below the reading grade level you are teaching. Grading Math and Science with a calculator or Teacher's Manual is allowed. You are not the person learning the material---you are grading work performed by someone else. It is not cheating.

Outlining is one of my most interesting pieces of teaching. Every once in awhile I assign one of the kids to outline a chapter they seem to have particular problems with. As a fourth grader in public school, I had a teacher who was insistent that we outline almost *everything*. In truth, she was probably assigning us one outline a week, but for me it was pure torture, and the reason became very clear to me while grading one of my son's Physical Science assignments last week. The textbook provided a format for outlining a major section of the preceding chapter as an assignment prepared for a day before a Unit Test. Of course, in my own little way, I panicked, and for a few minutes actually considered not making him do it, because I knew it would eat up about three pages of paper, and probably an hour of his time. Though my son offered to complete the entire test if he could beg off the outline, I wouldn't let him. I told him to prepare his outline. As I was grading his assignment, which he turned out to enjoy immensely and learned a great deal from (as witnessed by his test grade the next day), I discovered a passage which went something like this: (This is not a quote - I'm paraphrasing)

Compare your work with the others in your class to see the differences, because there is more than one way to outline this material. Remember no effort is really wrong unless it lists inaccurate information.

A light bulb went on in my head very suddenly. What I had hated about outlining for twenty seven years was not the outlining itself, but the way my fourth grade teacher presented it. She had a teacher's manual which she followed like a Bible, and expected us to interpret the material in the textbook exactly the way it was written - or it was wrong. That is a fallacy. My information was not necessarily inaccurate, and my listings weren't necessarily wrong. What was wrong was the assumption that my teacher had made in thinking that all of the outlines coming from her students had to be uniform. This, by the way, applies to lots of things. Always consider your child's interpretation of subject matter before deciding that answers are wrong. They may be partially wrong, or they may be perfectly right. Teacher's Editions aren't always perfect either.

In reviewing many of the texts my children have used over the past several years, I have found that there is no *perfect* text. For one reason or another all of the T.E.'s I have used have had mistakes - some occurring in the answer sections. Several times I have graded a relatively simple problem incorrect repeatedly before I worked the calculation myself and found that my child was correct the first time. It is important to me to apologize to the child when this happens. Sometimes ice cream helps...sometimes it doesn't. If an answer in the T.E. looks wrong or you suspect it is, work the problem yourself!

It is best, if you are unfamiliar with or uncomfortable with the subject matter to review the next section each day in that subject so that you have some time to sort through what you have learned and can present it to your child. If you have one available, teacher's guides will give you much of the confidence you need, because most will tell you verbatim what to tell the child if he or she becomes confused...but be careful, and remember what I said about point of view, editing problems, and interpretation earlier in the chapter.

-16-

CREATING YOUR OWN MATERIALS

"The beginning is half of every action."
Greek Proverb

Teachers create their own materials all the time, and there is no secret to it. I guess the only reason I feel that I should include this chapter in the book is because most of my friends who are considering home schooling ask me where I get my materials, and they know I can't purchase all the materials my children use.

My son's sixth grade teacher couldn't type. She actually made up all of her own worksheets and tests using cursive, which at times was almost illegible, which didn't matter when she was grading. The whole class just didn't get that question right. This does not imply that a legible worksheet or test can't be prepared in cursive by a parent, on a sheet of notebook paper. For home school, such workpapers may be just the ticket from time to time.

The worksheets the textbook companies prepare are generally of the following types:

✎Puzzles and word finds to increase vocabulary retention

✎Short vignette stories with four or five questions relative to the material studied in the textbook.

✎Twenty or so multiple choice, true/false, or fill-in questions on a single sheet.

I find that publications seldom prepare more than one worksheet per section of reading, and this seems to correspond with my theory that their plan is to provide approximately twenty minutes of work for the average student. The purpose of worksheets is to cement information that must be learned by rote, or to introduce information that could not otherwise be introduced in a format that is acceptable and readable to a child. My rule for worksheets for my youngest son, while he was studying on a Kindergarten level was to provide work at approximately a 16 point Arial Font, in **bold** which looks like this: (I use no more than five or six questions at a time, and with wide spacing - usually double spaced)

1.   The cat is a (green, white) cat.
2.   The dog is a (large, blue) dog.

The idea of this sort of work is to provide repetitious reading practice with an obvious choice so that the child can circle an answer without having to fill in a blank, since fine motor coordination (at least for him) had not kicked in as of yet.

On a first grade level, I remain in the same font type and size (font size (i.e., 16 pt.) is important, because it is tough for a little kid to distinguish words as separate entities if they are still struggling with identifying individual alpha-numerics. But for first grade level, when the fine motor starts to work, we produce something that looks like this

1.   The cat is a _____ cat.
(green/white)
2.   The dog is a _____ dog.
(large/blue)

We can now fit several more questions (up to 8 or 10) per sheet, and the child is required to not only circle the appropriate word, but to also fill in the blank. If the child writes *green* in the space that requires *white* in question #1, by the way, it doesn't necessarily mean that the child is stupid, it might indicate that your child has a sense of humor.

The basal readers we used when we first started working with our youngest did not provide additional vocabulary work, so I would write worksheets such as these quite often, and include many of the same sentences as possible, so that he look back to the book he was reading, and remember the structure of the sentences he had read.

This helps to increase not only vocabulary, phonics, and reading skills, but also encourages reading comprehension, which seems to be what is missing in many public school curriculums where children fail to read above a third grade level upon graduation.

Likewise, with Science, Social Studies, Math, or any other subject where you might need instant enrichment materials; keep in mind that in creating any worksheet for your child, you can provide whatever your child's individual situation requires. For example, when my six year old was working in his second grade math book, he was not provided space in his book to provide for his still undeveloped handwriting skills. He still made his numbers big. This also became a problem with worksheets provided by textbook companies as he progressed through his other programs. His reading skills were fine, but his handwriting looked like he was wearing mittens.

Starting with a 16 pt. (or larger) type font, in a very clear type style, like Arial, you are providing a clear portrait of the information. Make sure your work is neat and uncluttered, and do your best to spell properly. Working in 16 pt. bold Arial is kind of silly for a fifth or sixth grader, who is already reading in 12 point in most of his books anyway, so, logically, you can reduce the size of the type font according to the age and ability of your child. But remember, still, that there still has to be adequate room for your child to print, or later, use their new cursive skills adequately and clearly. You know how frustrating it is to try to fill in small boxes on a standardized form. It is equally as frustrating for a child.

Remember, when making up worksheets which relate to written information in the textbooks, it is probably a better idea to paraphrase rather than to copy information verbatim. Paraphrasing tests reading comprehension on a higher level.

I have included here biology study questions, to cover a day of reading and writing in biology. For each day, this high school level student is assigned approximately 13-14 pages of reading text and I have provided the comprehension questions because the textbook did not. This worksheet was presented as open-book and the student was asked to answer in short-answer format in a separate spiral notebook. As an alternative, answer lines may be provided so the work can be completed on the worksheet.

Biology Study Questions

Name_____ Date_____

Pages 2-15

1. Define "Nocturnal".
2. Give two reasons why being nocturnal is an advantage for some species.
3. Special Senses:
    a. How do rattlesnakes and pythons locate their prey in the darkness?
    b. Which of the senses are adapted in tigers so that they can survive in the dark?
    c. Describe briefly how changes such as these occur in species.
4. Define "echolocation".
5. How do owls locate their prey in the dark?
6. How do nightjars and nighthawks hunt insects?
7. Are hyenas scavengers, predators, or both?
8. What do wild boars eat?
9. How does a skunk defend itself?
    What does the liquid do to the intruder or enemy?
10. How do bats spend the daytime hours?
11. How do bats use echolocation?
12. How many pulses of sound per second are bats capable of producing?
    What do they do as they home in on their prey?
13. What do most bats eat?

Essay Question

Choose a family of nocturnal animals and highlight a defensive mechanism or adaptation which has made that family successful. Explain why this mechanism or adaptation is of value to that specific family in terms of the habitat or ecological niche that type of animal occupies.

In this way, you can test your child to see if he is comprehending what he has read. All of my worksheets and many but not all tests are given on an 'open book' format. This means that while they are completing the worksheet, they can look back at what they have previously read, find the information, and come up with their answer. This eliminates guessing, or, worse yet, creating a concrete memory for them of an incorrect answer. If you decide to follow my advice and insist on your child making corrections for every worksheet or test they complete, this will mean that they will encounter the information a number of different ways:

     1   They will read the information when they are assigned their initial reading assignment.

     2   They will encounter the information in a vocabulary exercise which will strengthen their usage.

     3   They will encounter the information when they are required to read through the information as they make their corrections.

     4   They will re-encounter the information a few days later when they have completed the chapter and they take their unit test.

     5   They will come across the information a fifth time when they make their corrections on their test. If they get 100% on the test, they can go on, confident that they have learned what they originally set out to learn for that lesson.

There are a number of software programs available for making crossword puzzles. I know people who use them, but I can't seem to get them to work in my machine. (Maybe I should have one of my kids load mine up for me!). I make crossword puzzles by hand with graph paper, a ruler, and cut and paste the clues either with my word processor or directly onto the same page with my typewriter. This goes fast for me. Whatever works for you is best. But they only take about a half hour to prepare the first time, and get easier after you get the hang of it.

I create my own word finds as follows---and we use a lot of them because in order to find a given word, your child has to repeat the spelling over and over in their head until the word pops out from the page.

Creating Word Finds

S	E	P	T	E	M	B	E	R	O
T	H	E	S	E	F	A	R	E	C
T	H	E	N	A	E	M	M	E	T
S	M	O	J	F	B	A	T	H	O
J	A	N	U	A	R	Y	E	M	B
U	R	O	L	P	U	O	N	T	E
N	C	V	Y	R	A	G	H	S	R
E	H	E		I	R		U		
	M		L	Y			S		
	B							T	
	D	E	C	E	M	B	E	R	
	R								

(The word find is only partially completed but gives you an idea of how a secret message can be easily incorporated for your child. Remember to finish fill-in the blank squares. Always provide a list of words for your child to find - no matter how obvious the list may be to you)

January	May	September
February	June	October
March	July	November
April	August	December

✔Determine your vocabulary from whatever source or word list that you come up with. I have, here used the names of the months, which would be a reasonable alternative spelling assignment for approximately third grade reading level. As stupid as this may sound for this particular exercise, write down a list of the words on a piece of scratch paper before you start, check your spelling, and determine the word with the largest number of letters.

January	May	September
February	June	October
March	July	November
April	August	December

✔Since September is the longest word here (9 letters), and for a twelve word list, I started with a 10x10 grid.

✔Word finds can easily be formed using a piece of notebook paper (If you're good at lining things up vertically, you may not need the ruler. If you need to, use it. You can follow the same directions I have below, deleting any instructions I have for completing the puzzle on the computer.

✔Because most word processing programs will attempt to line up your words (and in this case you will be using individual letters), you will have a problem if you don't use a grid or spread sheet layout, because you will be constantly fighting the computer's attempt to make your manuscript look right. You're not writing a letter - you're doing something that the word processor wasn't programmed for.

✔If you have decided to start with a 10x10 grid, pull it down, and then move the lines to the left until you have boxes that look approximately like squares on Page 76. You will only be putting one capital letter in each square, so you don't need much space. It is easier for the kids to find angled words if you have created something that approximates a square.

✔Remember that anything you put in the upper right hand corner is a give-away. I generally start my grid with a longer word with lots of different letters somewhere in the middle of the paper. In this case, I chose the word **January**, then chased down all the words in the list that fit easily with the word **January** vertically. Then I noticed that the angle formed between **February** and back to **April** gave me an opportunity to angle **August** down toward the right lower corner. When I got to **November**, I noticed that I was going to need two more squares (You noticed I ended up with a 10x12 grid, instead of a 10x10? You were right). I tabbed in two additional rows to fit **November** vertically, and ended up with additional space to fit **December** down on the second to the bottom row.

✔*Note:* When my son brought home a word find from school one day with two obviously obscene words in it, I became understandably concerned and called his teacher. At the ensuing parent teacher conference, we found that one of the students had created the word find, and claimed that he 'didn't realize' that he had 'inadvertently' included the words in his puzzle. But, this sort of thing does happen, and when it does, its embarrassing. So, my solution to that problem, is to make up a little extra credit assignment while I am filling in the 'filler' entries in between the letters of the puzzle. Be careful that you don't accidentally delete any of your puzzle words while you are filling it in with your message or fillers.

✔After the kids have circled all of the words, or better yet, used three highlighter pens and used one for horizontal, one for vertical and one for angled words; they can write down all the additional letters, which say "these are the names of the months". Of course, I would go on to fill in the rest of the grid with some other such uplifting and witty phrase, but it gives you an idea of how these things can be put together.

✔Of course, I would not use a partially composed grid as I have shown here for a student assignment. What I would do is finish out the puzzle, make the grid disappear (if your computer can do that), and you have a rectangle with lots of letters that looks amazingly like word find books in the bookstore, or exactly like those that the kids would find in a bound workbook.

✔Again, make sure that you include the list of the words in the puzzle, or the kids will be looking forever, trying to figure out how many words you shoved into this rectangle, and they can count through and stop when its time to stop. It gives them a good list to cross off with the appropriate highlighter color. Also, this will give them a clear message if you choose to include it.

Susanne L. Bain

POLLUTION WORD FIND

A	I	R	P	O	L	L	U	T	I	O	N	D	O	Y	O	W
H	S	U	P	R	O	T	E	C	T	S	E	E	L	T	H	A
E	T	N	O	I	S	E	P	O	L	L	U	T	I	O	N	T
A	R	E	L	M	E	E	S	S	A	I	G	E	T			E
L	A		L		E				V		E	T			R
T	Y		U		R		G	A	S	E	S	N	E			P
H	A		T	A							V	R			O
H	N		E			C	O	M	M	U	N	I	T	Y		L
A	I	H	D	E	X	H	A	U	S	T		R				L
B	M				H	E	A	L	T	H	Y	O				U
I	A					M					E	N				T
T	L					I		S		T		M				I
S	S					C	T		S	H		E	S			O
		C	L	E	A	N	A	I	R		N	M			N
	L				R	L	T			O		T	O		
		U				S				A			K		
		N		F	U	M	E	S	T			E		
		O	G			R	E	C	Y	C	L	E		
		S		S				L						
I	N	S	E	C	T	S				L					

Find these words in the puzzle above:

rats	healthy	clean air	environment
live	exhaust	recycle	noise pollution
hear	smoke	chemicals	health habits
see	lungs	smell	air pollution
nose	protect	insects	community
gases	taste	litter	water pollution
fumes	throat	polluted	stray animals

✔Make a copy of the first puzzle you make, before you fill in your message or add letters as fill-ins, or you will end up spending as much time as the kids trying to find the words your child can't find. Use different colored highlighters to mark the words you have hidden. This will be your answer key. In a list of twelve words, its not nearly as important as doing this when you have fifty or one hundred words for your child to find and for you to grade.

Tests can be created similarly and in a format much like the worksheets you have created for the daily reading sections. Generally, a textbook is set up for four to six daily assignments and a test. If you think that you will be able to give all your tests on Friday, remember that unless that works particularly well for you and your children, testing one section and giving daily assignments in the rest of the course work will be create less stress for your child and yourself, and you will not end up with an exhausted child at the end of the day. Testing does not mean that you are not teaching for that day.   In general, most tests for grades two through five are printed in a moderately large font (a little bigger than 12 pt.) and consist of no more than two pages. Reasonable testing for sixth on up can probably consist of about three pages in 12 pt.

I like to create a mix in my children's tests. All true and false, all multiple choice, or all essay probably won't work for most subjects. Even math tests can include multiple choice and true/false questions. I generally give a mix of about ten true/false, ten multiple choice with four choices each, and three or four essay questions per test for my daughter at a 4/5 grade level, and double that number for an eighth grade level, just simply because there is more information to review in the upper grade levels. Also, upper grade levels tend to make their chapters much longer and schedule testing about every ten lessons.

Limiting the number of questions can be a problem, so what I concentrate on while making the tests is the information that the child seemed to have problems with as they were working through the daily assignments. Sometimes I can create a test for that child in that unit with only that information, and sometimes, I add additional review questions just to keep them alert (and also give them the satisfaction of being able to intuitively know an answer without having to think it out or look it up.)

One thing is true, if you can obtain copies of work-and test-

Life Science Exam

Name_____   **Date** _____

Life Science - Cells and Structures

You have been given a diagram of two different kinds of cells. One of them is an animal cell and the other is a plant cell. First, locate the name of the portion of the cell or cells that the arrow points to, and put the letter and the name of that part on the line provided on the diagram. Second, find the purpose this portion of the cell serves for the plant and/or animal in which the cell works.

A.	Plant Cell	1___	Provides shape and support for some cells.
B.	Animal Cell	2___	Contains material that forms the code that controls cell activity.
C.	Chloroplast	3___	Where proteins are made.
D.	Endoplasmic Reticulum	4___	Controls movement of materials into and out of the cell.
E.	Cell Wall	5___	Moves materials within cells.
F.	Nucleus	6___	Controls movement of materials into and out of the nucleus.
G.	Mitochondria	7___	Stores and releases chemicals.
H.	Vacuole	8___	Releases energy. The powerhouse of the cell.
I.	Ribosome	9___	This is a cell of a typical plant and not how *all plant* cells will look under a microscope.
J.	Cell Membrane	10___	Stores water and dissolved materials.
K.	Golgi Bodies	11___	Contains a variety of cell structures.
L.	Cytoplasm	12___	This is a cell of a typical animal and not how *all animal* cells will look under a microscope.
M.	Chromosomes	13___	Contains chlorophyll, which traps light used in making food.
N.	Nuclear Membrane	14___	Carry the code that controls a cell.

Life Science Exam - Page Two
Parts of the Cell - Please Label the Diagram

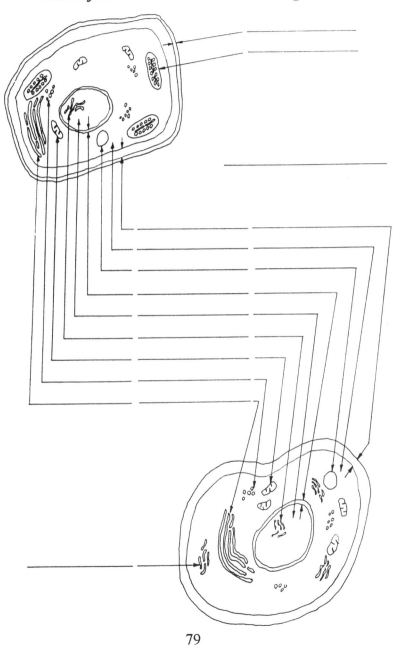

Life Science Exam - Page Three

Data and Observations

Cell Part	Location	Function
Cell Membrane		
Nucleus		
Cytoplasm		
Cell Wall		
Endoplasmic Reticulum		
Ribosomes		
Golgi Bodies		
Mitochondria		
Chloroplasts		
Chromosomes		

Life Science Exam - Page Four

Life Science - Cells and Structures - Essays

1. What structures are found in the plant cell that are not found in the animal cell?

_____

_____

_____

2. Which diagram is the plant cell?_____

3. How can you tell?_____

_____

_____

4.   Look at the plant specimens under your microscope again, and see if you can draw a diagram in the space below of the clearest of your plant specimens. See if you can identify any or all of the parts identified in diagram B on Page 52 of your text. Then, look at the blood specimen, bring it into the highest focus and see if you can identify any of the parts identified in diagram A on Page 52. Draw a diagram on the back of this page of what you see in the microscope and label the parts. Take your time and play around with the objectives and different levels of focus and the different distances from the stage to the objective.

booklets with answers for the textbooks you are using, it cuts down a great deal on the amount of time you must spend as a parent preparing additional materials, although this exercise can be fun and more comprehensive.

I am reminded (as I always am as I prepare projects for my children) of a young mother and Kindergarten level teacher who lived near us when we lived in the mountains of Colorado. I had recently given birth to my first son, and was home, operating my small secretarial service when I received a knock at my door. Sandy (not her real name) was in tears. She had returned to school after the summer and discovered that a second Kindergarten teacher had been hired, and was assigned to the classroom next to hers. As she had been preparing the classroom for her new students, Sandy had stepped into the next classroom and discovered that some of the ideas she had posted the previous day were copied in the classroom next door. Instead of being flattered, she was outraged and furious because *'her projects'* had been *'stolen'*. I sat with her as she cried her eyes out, and pretended to be patient and understanding as I thought about how sad things had become when experienced teachers were incapable of mentoring new teachers. Isn't sharing an important part of the Kindergarten curriculum?

If the teachers in our public school systems can't cooperate and share with one another, how are they to teach our children to cooperate and share? These are, by the way, the major functions of the kindergarten teacher, are they not?

Because this was one of the first exposures that I had to the 'new attitude' of this type of selfish teacher, I have been stunningly aware of the repetition of this type of attitude among my children's teachers. As a home schooling parent, I hope that I can share as much of what I find to work as I possibly can--and continue to do so---and I hope that any other home schooling parent I meet will be similarly forthcoming. I have found most to be so, so far. I wish you and your children the best education you and your friends can possibly offer!

-17-

TEACHING MATH

"I am not afraid of storms for I am learning how to sail my ship."
Louisa May Alcott

One of the biggest sources of concern regarding home schooling comes from moms who stress with the very idea of teaching math to their children. I find this interesting, because I believe I have never met a dad who was unwilling to help a child with Math. I discovered why when my daughter came home one day and told me that her best friend in second grade (a boy) was given extra work in Math, while she was working on something else (an art project).

Interested and understandably curious, I started to explore the concept that there was a possibility that teachers have historically actually discouraged girls and young women in their classroom teaching methods. I firmly believe this is true.

My children's grandmother, as well, explained that "I never did well in Math, either, dear, so don't worry about it. I turned out all right." This was unfortunate for her, but not a philosophy I would choose for my children, nor was it appropriate, since my daughter was doing fine in math! It seems lots of people are going around telling little girls that they don't have to learn Math and Science. Why? Because they perceived that they didn't do well themselves. There is no reason for this other than prevalent social attitude and peer pressure, and no reason that little girls and little boys cannot absorb the same material at roughly the same pace. I know too many female Accountants, Attorneys, Engineers, Architects and Doctors to even partially believe this myth.

The problem, then, is not that women cannot learn math. It is that we have been programmed since infancy to think that for some reason we are stupid when it comes to numbers. Why? We all have the same number of fingers and toes, but we are encouraged to use manipulatives and fingers, and boys are forced to memorize and remember formulas. Guess what? In some ways, it is easier for us as women, because we must apply so much of what we use intuitively to the everyday, mundane chores that we perform for our families every day. Ever use a recipe intended for a family of four to make dinner for a family of five, six, ten, or a group of twenty five? My husband wouldn't want to, and neither, probably would yours. But you can. Have you ever had to buy groceries? Do you pay household bills? I do, and I'm sure you do as well.

Fractions, for example, are easily taught. Draw two circles and tell your five year old child to split the first one into however many pieces you want him to portray. Its probably best to ask for four or five pieces at first. This first effort will probably have pieces of different sizes. Now, tell your child to pretend that the circle is a pie, and ask him to color or point to the one piece he would like to have. I would be willing to wager that the piece chosen was the biggest piece. Now, tell your child to look at the second circle and split it into the same number of pieces, making believe that it is a pie (or cake---just make sure it is something he or she likes), then tell him that his friends will choose first (you can name the friends if it helps), and that he could end up with any of the pieces on his chart. He will probably give you a pretty close facsimile of a perfectly segmented circle for use in fractions.

Another permutation of the same game: If Timmy and Sara take two pieces they are taking 2 of 5 pieces or 2/5. There are 3 of five pieces left, or 3/5. 2+3=5, so there you have it. 5/5. In this example, you have a simple word problem, easily explained with a circle and a crayon.

Rudimentary addition and subtraction (probably to ten) can also be taught with crayons. I use crayons for lots of things because uncoordinated little fingers can move them around. Get much above ten, and you have too many crayons to keep track of. This is when you can switch to a number line. I use the cm side of a ruler for this. Rulers are portable and easy to keep track of, and it is good practice for the eventual teaching of Algebra which almost prescribes an innate

Multiplication Table

	0	1	2	3	4	5	6	7	8	9	10	11	12
0													
1													
2													
3													
4													
5													
6													
7													
8													
9													
10													
11													
12													

understanding of moving along number lines. Better yet, tired little hands don't have to draw a new number line for each problem. They look for their rulers. Enough adding on the ruler, and the child will, by definition, memorize answers if he sees the problems often enough. But the repetition has to be daily (on work days---not weekends), and cannot progress beyond your child's developmental readiness---don't advance to the next set of problems until he knows one set of addition and understands it....its gets easier and easier for them!

Multiplication tables can be simplified in a number of ways, and once learned, makes it very easy to move onto division:

✔We have a number of games that we play (hide and seek/Marco Polo) where the seeker has to hide their eyes and count. You don't have to count by ones, twos or tens. A child can also count from 1 to 35 by 7's. Or 1 to 27 by 3's. Or 1 to 81 by 9's. Get it? "Counting by's" can be used early-on as rudimentary preparation for multiplication tables. My six year old could count by any number through ten, by 20's, 25's and 100's by the end of the summer, when he was barely five. Keeping up with older siblings encourages little kids to think fast and remember.

✔When introduced to the first page of multiplication problems, some children panic. They don't have to. This may be a reflection of a parent's reaction. My first lesson in multiplication for my daughter last year was to copy a multiplication table. That was her only assignment for the whole day, and she completed it rather quickly, but got several of the numbers wrong. This was good, because it gave me the opportunity for her to learn how the table worked by re-constructing the chart under my supervision, to follow horizontal and vertical columns with her fingers. Of course, you may wish to buy or create a table for your child on your computer. Try starting with a table that only goes to fives. Zeros, ones, twos and fives are easiest. Threes are next, because most kids can count by threes. Fours can be easily figured out.

✔While completing homework in the next few days, allow your child to use the multiplication table that she or he has created. **Don't make the table yourself, because you will be defeating the purpose**. If the table is lost, the child must re-create it. Re-creating the table will get easier as your child memorizes the facts. Believe me, the table will disappear within about a month and your child will never need it again **if you provide practice every day**.

✔Even if your child is studying something else in math, make sure that for three to five months that he or she is repeatedly exposed to multiplication problems (and, if ready, division.) That is where the *Mad Minutes®* come in handy, because this book creates repetitive practice. Additionally, *Essential Learning Products Company* publishes a series of small format exercise books which gently take the kids through a year of multiplication, division, subtraction, addition, decimals, metric, or fractional equations in non-threatening and understandable format.

There is always an easy way to teach each challenging subject, and you might be surprised that, with the additional practice that your every day life has produced, Math does not produce the type of fear you anticipate it might. Give yourself a chance to feel comfortable with your teaching methods in other subjects, and that will give you confidence to tackle Math, Reading, English, or whatever you perceive your weakness to be. In any course, a step-by-step approach is best for both student and teacher, and allows both to absorb information before moving on to the next concept. In this way, both student and teacher can share the learning experience, and, in addition, enrich both lives.

Comments I have received while mentoring workshops indicate that mothers who at first feel uncomfortable teaching math gain confidence more quickly if they havemoved from rudimentary math or arithmetic through the upper level math programs of Algebra and beyond. This is because as they are working with their children their personal skills are being enhanced and built upon to a point where the material in the upper level texts seems clearer than their first exposure while in high school or even college. This has also been my personal experience. As adults we can learn and grow through teaching.

-8-

CRAYONS AND LITTLE KIDS

"When our children show us one of their creations, they are usually trying to tell us something, not create a work of art, and they will get the most encouragement for going on when we show them that we care about what they are trying to say."
Fred Rogers

As nutty as it sounds, the first SUCCESSFUL teaching experiences I had with my five year old when we began home schooling the second time around were with crayons. Most children are familiar with crayons. Anyone not isolated on a desert island since WW2 is familiar with crayons. We are given crayons everywhere we go in restaurants, and if you are willing to carry them in your purse (not a good idea in really hot weather--and keep them off the car seat and out of pockets!), you can quickly make your collection really big.

My best suggestion, though, is this: go and buy a small box of ten primary and secondary color crayons. The ones with red, blue, yellow, green, black, purple....not the ones that say things like mauve, pine green, or blue aster on the wrappers, and not the ones that are packaged as multi-cultural, because they will only be natural skin colors, and will not be applicable for this practice, though they are fun for coloring books. Also, while you are at it, you might consider getting the big box with the sharpener in it, and tuck it away as a terrific surprise (and besides, one time in each of our lives, we should have the big box with the sharpener in it). With the little box, though, you can do all the things I describe below. My little box, by the way, was packaged along with the big box, shrink wrapped at a *back to school* sale.

Crayons are good for little fingers. It is hard for little children to grip for a variety of reasons. The paper cover on a crayon is important in that it provides something to hold on to. Don't let your child destroy the points on your primary set and tear back the paper--- make sure they use another set to color in coloring books with (maybe the big box with the sharpener I mentioned). What we are preserving here is the original tip so that if they need to write they have a good point, and, most importantly, the simple color name on the crayon.

Find a coloring book at the grocery store (or wherever) that has the names of the colors within the patterns on the pages. Some of the rack-sold workbooks at department stores, toy stores and teaching supply stores feature beautiful, simple designs for this very purpose. Start with the ones in which few colors are mentioned. Help your child to correctly identify where to read the words on the crayons and where to read the words in the pictures in the book. If you can't find a book with the colors pre-printed into the design, you might consider taking a non-smear black pen and very carefully and neatly printing the colors into the design of one or more of the pictures in a simplistic coloring book or on pictures you've drawn (if you're artistic and good at one-line drawings) to achieve the same effect.

You would be surprised to know that your child may be operating under the mistaken impression that no word is spelled the same way twice. Or, put another way, they may think language is constructed for each individual usage of a word. Explain that green, the color, is always, always was, and always will be spelled g-r-e-e-n. Likewise with r-e-d, y-e-l-l-o-w, b-l-u-e, b-l-a-c-k, and so on. This is important as it establishes spelling continuity. It will surprise you how quickly your child will turn to your husband and read these words out of context. Teaching your child spelling continuity will eliminate a lot of headaches you didn't know you might have had when your child later tries to sound out what should be considered sight words. It happens. Let me reiterate:

Teach your child that words are spelled the same all the time. Spellings do not change.

After your child has mastered the color-name coloring book exercises, you might go in search of the coloring books that indicate a color by number. How do you explain this process? Well, the 7 is right next to the word y-e-l-l-o-w that he learned a few days ago, and still corresponds to the same color name on the crayon, and he will probably catch on very quickly.

You may find some coloring books which indicate color preference with a series of dots. This requires additional pre-math skills, but if he or she is willing; it, too, is relatively easy to teach. You might also find some interesting paint by number books with the color pigment for watercoloring impregnated into the paper. While this is messy, it serves much the same purpose, and provides another alternative, and yet another opportunity to notice that g-r-e-e-n still spells green!

Teaching a little person to count is easy and fun, too. I started by taking my children out to the swingset and counting consecutive numbers each time I pushed them in the swing. Normally, this is a very boring thing to do, but first I would count to ten, for a few times, then to twenty for a few times, just to get them used to a regular rhythm. Remember at this early part of their development, you are best to start by counting by 1's. Try this for a couple of days. **Note**: This method will also work for an older child, while doing repetitive things with your child and teaching them to count by 2's, 3's, 4's, 5's, etc.---but as I said, with a young child, don't confuse him by skipping numbers, or he won't figure out the sequencing.

Go inside the house and write the numbers one to ten on a piece of paper, and let your child count to ten, while you point to the numbers. Once he starts to recognize the numbers, get a simple dot to dot book. On the first page, write the numbers in order. (Hopefully you have a dot book that starts out with 1-10 so you will not need to write many numbers, your child need not understand many numbers to get started, and so that you can work up to larger numbers gradually). Make your numbers just as legible and pretty close to the same shape as the numbers in the dot book. Help your child with the first pattern. He may need additional help, but pretty soon, he will be asking for another puzzle, because, even as obvious as the picture may be to you, he will be surprised; at least with the initial pictures.

It is after this point where, if you need to do so, you may use a ruler instead of your mom-made number line, because soon you child will be going to number 30, at which time, it is important to point out that 0-9 repeats over and over again in the one's place, and that other numbers appear in the 10's place as you reach 0 again. Using this method, you will teach only through 30, because a 12"/cm ruler only goes to 30 cm. This process helps to teach place-value, which later becomes important, and may be a little more difficult to teach once the kids get up into higher-value numbers in their 3rd and 4th grade Math programs.

Prepare your child for number study early, and they will think they have always understood mathematics in an easy and very natural way.

When you get ready to start adding and subtracting (as I mentioned in my last chapter), simply take your still-in-good shape set of ' Mom won't let me use these' crayons, and teach addition to ten and subtraction up to *from ten* problems. These should serve as the only manipulatives you need. They're inexpensive, and can be found anywhere.

If you feel that you need a bunch of manipulatives, remember pennies are relatively inexpensive to use, although they tend to roll when on their sides, and can be hard to pick up. Crayons roll, but are easier to handle. Colorful little bears and pigs and things they sell at teaching supply stores are cute, but quite expensive. Look around and see if you can find anything in your house that you have lots of. Dried pinto beans and macaroni shells work wonderfully well. I made it a point to experiment with my youngest son, and not use manipulatives in any way once he had gotten past 1-10 addition and subtraction, and he is doing perfectly well.

When working with a number line in addition, always tell your child to start counting with the larger of the two numbers. Explain that in addition problems, you can start adding with either of the two numbers. This concept will carry through for him later in Algebra. Many children get to the 8th Grade without really realizing that 8+9=9+8! So, for example, if you are adding 7+5, start by placing your finger on the 7 on the ruler, then count up five more numbers (say "here is 7---let's count another five--then point to the 8 and say "one", the nine and say "two", etc; until you get to 12, where you say "five". This is where you get all happy and say "See? Seven plus five equals twelve!") This is not nearly as confusing as it sounds, and it will help your child a great deal even in two and three digit addition problems in which they must deal with carries.

The number line theory also works with subtraction. For 8-2, for example you start at 8, by placing your finger on the "8" on the ruler, then count back "One", "Two"--this is where you get all happy and say "See? Eight minus two equals six!" **Remember**, though, since you explained that you start with the bigger number first in addition, that your child has it stuck in his/her mind that you can interchange the numbers in all math problems, and this is not true. But since, in both cases you have started with the larger of two numbers, that is ok, for our purposes here. At some point, you have to drop the bomb that you can't manipulate the numbers in subtraction problems and obtain proper results, unless you wish to teach negative numbers to a second grader.

I would strongly recommend obtaining Teacher's Editions for your children's upper level mathematics textbooks, because if you don't have them, you must calculate answers the same way as your child does....which is by working the problems. This is not your job, it is your child's. If you do not have a Teacher's Edition, with problem solutions, it will probably take quite a bit longer to grade math, and you might grow to resent the time you spend, and be tempted to assign less problems. This may result in less practice for your child. This isn't necessarily a good idea, because your children really need the practice, so it is wise to try to obtain the best possible textbooks for math. Remember, sometimes the answers in the teacher's editions are incorrect. Double-check if you are in doubt.

Saxon Math provides either a full-fledged Teacher's Edition in hardbound, or a Home School Edition, which comes with a Notebook-sized paper backed edition which lists only answers. This works fine, unless your child misses an answer and you have to figure out why. This is, by the way, what you will probably need to do anyway, if you wish to give your child guidance. In most cases, your student will come back to you for an explanation if she is confused.

In the past, I did not allow my children to use calculators for their math. This was true, even for my son, who was doing upper level math. This was for the simple reason that I did not, my husband did not, and neither did anyone who learned math previous to 1975 or so. We used sliderules. I felt strongly that using a calculator was like allowing children to continue counting on their fingers. The calculator does not need to be educated, nor does it need the practice. Your child's mind does require education, and therefore, it is best to allow his or her mind to work for her or him. To a certain extent, I still feel much the same way. I still want my children to be able to calculate the cost of purchase quickly using their own intelligence. This helps at places like car dealerships, computer warehouses, and grocery stores.

What changed my attitude was the SAT exam, in which each student was allowed, and therefore used, a sophisticated math/science calculator, such as a TI83 Graphing Calculator. Make sure that as your child approaches Algebra and Geometry that he or she learns to properly use such a calculator, so that you do not need to quickly teach the use of such equipment immediately before your child is tested. Without the calculator, scores for your child will not properly reflect your child's potential since those results will not reflect their use of the same technology as the other students are using. This will place your child at a disadvantage, so make sure the skills are in place many months previous to testing.

-19 -

TELEVISION

"Power can be seen as power with rather than power over, and it can be used for competence and co-operation, rather than dominance and control."
Anne L. Barstow

We subscribe to what we believe to be one of the most expensive cable television services in the country---as a matter of fact, we have been told that it is the most expensive in Arizona. We do so because we believe that limiting our children's tv watching to PBS can be rather tedious. We not only subscribe to expensive cable, we subscribe to one of the most expensive packages that our cable company offers. Why? Because by subscribing to the more expensive cable package, we can receive the best that cable has to offer - i.e., upgraded and useful educational programming.

We are home with our children probably 90% of the time. We know precisely what our children are doing probably 98 to 99% of the time. We know what they watch on television, we set limits, and we enforce them. If we weren't here with them, we couldn't enforce this. If we didn't insist on absolute power over their television viewing we would lose control of what they were thinking through what they could conceivably be exposed to. I generally listen to my children as I work. I also stop my work frequently to watch the children do whatever they are doing. By noticing these important facets of their lives, I believe that I have made a difference for them.

Our children do not study their prescribed curriculum twenty four hours a day, nor do I expect to spend twenty four hours a day grading their work or answering questions. There has to be something else. This gap is filled with exercise, play, enrichment activities, television, and their time with their computers.

Despite the fact that I am actively fighting much of the type of programming offered on the major networks and many of the cable channels, I am gratified by the fact that there is so much available that is enriching that my family doesn't have to sink to that level at any time during the day. As a parent, it pays to keep up with what is available and shop for your children's programming.

My sister called me last week and asked me if I knew if Mister Rogers was still on television. At this time, of course he is! I only hope that he continues offering his wonderful brand of non-threatening, helpful discourse for many more years. He's on PBS and as of this time, you don't need cable to receive him. But what about the other twenty three and a half hours during the day, and what if your child is over the age of six?

The Discovery Channel, The Learning Channel, The History Channel, CSPAN, CNN, and **Disney,** as well as a number of other special interest, information-packed channels provide meaningful programming. Many of the other networks offer non-violent and uplifting programming throughout the week because they are required to do so. Community programming is often quite interesting and provides a refreshing alternative from time to time. Watch with your children to make sure that they are not exposed to advertising or programming that you do not anticipate or agree with. Be especially careful with your younger children if you become wrapped up in afternoon programming on the major networks. Sometimes parents forget their children are with them and can become inadvertently caught up in programming not meant for children.

My oldest son, for example, has developed a marked interest in Science Fiction, and, in particular *Star Trek*. His interest has sparked several learning experiences for him. For example:

✔Several years ago, he wanted to go to the theater and see *Jurassic Park*. With that request, and because we had already owned the book for two years, he was required to read his first immensely long (in his estimate) novel before he could see the film. Since then, he has branched out and can and will read any adult-length, adult-vocabulary text or novel he wants to read. (Yes, we remember to screen the literature!!!!)

✔He asked for nothing but Star Trek Technical Manuals for the holidays and his birthday one year. (That's not all he got, though). He quickly memorized them. Not important, other than the fact, that because he has spent much of his spare time re-drawing the diagrams to make the facilities more human-sized and usable, he has developed his drafting skills to the extent that he has made several design modifications to items that we have owned, drawn them up, and prepared them for publication, presentation, or patent.

✔He has designed and put together a technically correct and intricate board game complete with rules, using his knowledge of the universe (gained through reading Carl Sagan), and Micro-Machines. His game is now ready for patent and sale for manufacture.

✔He has designed and drafted shuttle crafts pixel by pixel on his computer, using information he has learned from studying current designs he picked up in his reading and having visited Cape Canaveral during our last two vacations to Florida.

That is not to say that my son is unusually gifted, but rather to indicate what is possible when you have an interested and enthusiastic student. All of this spawned from an interest in science fiction and watching 'too much *Star Trek*'.

We have rules governing television viewing in our home. Our children may turn on only certain channels, and certain things must be completed before the television goes on. If the rules are broken, that child does not watch for a week. Period. End of Discussion.

TV Advertising is probably the single most important reason to avoid network television. Much of it is obnoxious. Most commercials use improper grammar and overuse slang (pay attention next time, and it will make you laugh!). Many advertisers use subliminal hype, and most advertising agencies will utilize either violence or sex to sell anything. They cheat. It is harder to make a clean commercial with a witty message. I can admire those people, even though I prefer my children be influenced by real need than perceived or coerced desire.

-*20*-

COMPUTERS

"I do not think that I will ever reach a stage when I will say, 'This is what I believe. Finished.' What I believe is alive...and open to growth."
Madeleine L'Engle

If you have the resources at all, find the most up to date computer equipment you can buy. There is no doubt that PC's are absolutely necessary for any future your children will experience. With the advent of Windows and MacIntosh, it is virtually impossible for anyone not to understand exactly how to work with a computer from opening the box to creating whatever it is that a person needs to create.

New computers are easy to work with. When I learned about computers at the university in 1977, I worked with a mainframe the size of my house, and a stack of cards that, when dropped, became a pile of garbage impossible to sort out. There are no longer cards, just keyboards and lots and lots of instructions and lots of resources for questions. If you have problems learning to use your new computer, ask your kids to read the directions. Anyone over the age of 8 who has ever worked with any type of computer in the past five years can teach you---even if it is the fellow at the computer store who is aching to show off what he knows. (Little does he know that within two or three hours you will probably know at least as much as he does.) My message is, don't let them scare you, let them work for you and for your children. Believe me, the investment is well worth it, and the time you devote learning to teach your children with a computer will be a wonderful investment in yourself and in your children.

For anyone who doesn't already know, there are two basic considerations to buying computers.

The **hardware**, which consists of a **box** with all the **chips** in it or **central processing unit**, the **screen**, which shows you what you are doing, a **keyboard**, where you type in letters and numbers, a **mouse**, which directs the cursor all over the place on the screen and enables children who don't know how to read to do almost anything, and a **printer**, which, of course, prints out whatever you want to print when you tell it to. If you don't know anything about computers, I would strongly suggest that you buy everything as a set from a reputable dealer---someone that a friend or business associate has bought from, and who carries a viable and long-lasting warrantee. It is wise to opt for the additional extended warrantees offered by many electronic warehouse stores, because it indicates a willingness to work with you after the sale. You also know these people well enough to walk back in with your cpu under your arm and ask them to fix it for you.

Software consists of all the stuff that makes all the chips, screen, keyboard, mouse, printer and your directions interact. Most computer packages come with Software Packages. Look for a computer with an innate ability to do Word Processing (so you can write stories, poems, charts, assignment sheets, worksheets, and keep records), possibly accounting (if you want to use it to keep track of your expenses for tax purposes), and an Encyclopedia (for obvious reasons). I have yet to find a typing tutorial that is not insulting and rude, and any games that they give away with the computer will probably take about two weeks for your kids to figure out. Don't worry about the games. Consider it practice with the mouse and the keyboard. Eventually, if you give your kids time to mess around with them (again, set limits!), they will get bored with them. But, **this is important - remember to limit the time you or each of your children spend on the computer to less than two hours per day,** whether you are playing games or doing accounting. Many people are arguing about this issue right now, but to be safe, know how much time your children spend. Many hours in front of a computer screen every day does things to your eyes, your shoulders, your neck, your back, and your stomach. Don't let that happen to you!

Spend some time with your new computer to acclimate

yourself and your family to the software you already have before deciding to stock up on additional programs. If you wish, and you have purchased the computer and the software at the same place, you might be able to return to the place of purchase and have the software loaded by one of their staffers for a nominal price or for free. Remember to back-up, or copy all of the software on your computer to discs before you use any of it. If something happens and your operating systems are destroyed, it can be re-loaded by someone who knows what they are doing - again, with your warrantee, the place where you bought your computer in the first place.

It is very easy to spend tremendous amounts of money and in-computer hard storage on computer software. There are some wonderful learning programs available. Make sure you purchase from a reputable dealer and manufacturer, and make sure that the companies you are dealing with have a 1-800 number in case you run into problems. We loaded some software into my son's computer a few months ago which lunched everything on his computer - even the operating systems had to be replaced. Fortunately we had backed up the system and were able to return the mainframe box to the store where we purchased everything and have all of our software re-entered. We threw away the software that destroyed the insides of the computer, but I know that this happened many times to many people with this program even after the first complaints came back on their 1-800 line. I'm sure by now you've heard other horror stories.

Keep in mind that if you purchase your computer at a reduced price from an disreputable dealer, from an ad in the newspaper, or even from a friend or co-worker, there are a few things to consider. First, make sure that your computer and each of its components and software packages (each, individually, because you may be dealing with a dozen different manufacturers) is registered to you and in your name. It is illegal to copy software and give it to someone else. (Its also illegal to copy pages from a book and sell them---it falls under the same heading in the copyright office). If you are not the registered owner of the software or the hardware in the computer you have purchased, and you attempt to call the 1-800 number, they will know that you are not a registered owner. They may be unhappy that you have copied their work. Imagine purchasing a computer, having a piece of virused software destroy your operating system and needing to find someone to bring your computer back on line. You've now lost all the work stored inside your computer. It could happen.

Which brings us to another point. You may wish to store your children's grades, attendance reports, worksheets and tests in your computer (not to mention your tax records, poetry, recipes and medical records). Back up your system to discs regularly and store this information somewhere safe - a shelf in a closet works well. The manual that comes with your operating system will show you an easy way to do this. After all, it was the first thing you had to do when you bought your computer in the first place. If you have all this information stored on discs, in a plastic box up in someone's closet, you can pull it out and re-insert it after your operating systems have been restored. This forethought can mean the difference between a boo-boo and a logistical tragedy.

In my first book, I advised parents to avoid the **Internet** , however, with the advances we have made sociologically and the excellent filters available for families, I can safely say that one of the primary sources we now use in our family for current information and research is now our internet access. Easy to use, the internet can serve the needs of all of the members of your family, while providing your children with practical tools they will later need for successful entry into the professional position they will likely assume as adults.

I would strongly suggest that if your family has the opportunity to do so, to purchase a computer and encourage the children to use software, learn proper keyboarding techniques and take advantage of the vast array of information available through internet technology.

-*21*-

COMPLETING ASSIGNMENTS

"I do not know anyone who has got to the top without hard work. That is the recipe. It will not always get you to the top, but should get you pretty near."
Margaret Thatcher

One of the most common comments I hear from my friends who ask me about home schooling is
how do you get the kids to work?
My answer to this is: I tell them they have to.

We do not have a democracy in our house. We operate a benevolent monarchy. We love our children, but we are not, and do not pretend to be their best friends. We are structure that they can turn to, and we are there for them no matter what happens. We back them up, and we expect the truth from them. We expect them to perform their duties around the house. They take care of the animals, and in return, they do not receive an allowance - they are rewarded with love and devotion from the pets. They vacuum the floor, clean their rooms, and help with meals because they are asked to, and because they know that in return, my husband and I also are required to do many things that may seem in some ways rather unfulfilling, but that they create a loving and cohesive household where we do things for each other. They also know they are receiving an education, which they perceive as something valuable.

When we first started home schooling, I had particular difficulty with my daughter. I had few problems with my sons. My oldest son was so grateful not to have chairs pulled out from under

101

him, that he just enjoyed basking in the attention of having a teacher on call to answer questions. My youngest son had never attended school, and was looking forward to reading at the age of five. These are normal, healthy attitudes.

My daughter, however, loved public school. This is also a normal, healthy attitude. And she also lacked a certain respect for my intelligence. It took about four months of working with her to prove that I knew what I was doing, and that I was happy to help her with her work, as long as she could embrace it. As the year went by and she far surpassed the goals she had set for herself, she accepted that what we were doing was okay, and that she was learning at as fast a rate as she could with nobody to hold her back. She recognized that she was learning according to her own parameters. She finished two school grades in several subjects in a period of nine months. I didn't expect her to. This was not part of a plan. That is just how things worked out.

In short, we expect our children to do their work. We explain in no uncertain terms what we expect. We offer them an opportunity to excel, and to move as fast as their minds can take them

We quickly established Assignment sheets (similar to a teacher's planning book) for each of the older kids, listing the minimum work expected in columnar, easy to read form. I do not prepare a monthly or weekly lesson plan. Each of the kids has some sort of assignment in each subject each day. (Other parents do other things---this works for us, so don't let my ideas put you off.) Each assignment is graded each day, and the kids are expected to correct all of their mistakes from the previous day before they prepare the assignment for the next day. We do not let them move on if they are stuck somewhere - we offer enrichment material, or spend some time reviewing the material until they understand the material perfectly before we move on. This does not happen in a public school----how can a teacher possibly do this for 25 or more students each day?

Within each of their assignments, they usually have some pages in the textbooks to read and questions of some sort to answer on paper --be it experiments in science, essay questions in their spiral notebooks, or workbook pages. Each of these assignments is graded every day. This takes me approximately four hours to complete for the two older children. I check spelling very closely, and if there is a spelling error, whether in English or in their Foreign Language, they are required to write the word five times in their vocabulary book. If the word is used improperly, they must look it up and copy the definition from the Dictionary. In addition, we utilize a standardized spelling book separate and apart from our vocabulary list. Using this method, my son scored his highest marks on his ITBS in Usage, where he had a below grade level score while in the public school.

My youngest son, at ages 4-6 received my absolute and total attention (with interruptions from the other two kids only occasionally ---it was a matter of honor with them) for about two and a half hours each morning. He worked on Math, Phonics, Vocabulary, English usage and Reading. He was the only one of our three children using a prepared curriculum from a local Home School/Private School curriculum producer. Using *Horizon® Math and Phonics* we were able to put him at a *public school* third grade reading level, and a second grade math level in a period of about 9 months. He loved his work and wouldn't trade his time with me for anything. He has told me so. We added Science and Social Studies texts when he had completely finished his phonics work, so that he was not put off by the vocabulary...although he was reading much on his own already. He quickly mastered the first and second grade material, and within about five months he was ready for third grade level science and social studies; as well as a rudimentary introduction to Spanish as a foreign language. The whole process was quick, pleasant and predictable.

So, how *do* we get them to work? We promise them that they can go outside and play when they are finished, and the rest takes care of itself. One of my big problems is to pull them out of their extra work to get them outside. You may not be aware of this, but there are some interesting things in textbooks. If you choose the right ones, they are written so that children will be interested in them, since children are naturally curious! Knowledge ownership in and of itself can be quite seductive, and the possession of knowledge encourages humans to seek greater amounts of it, unless social pressure or other negative climate dissuades or circumvents this natural trait. It is correct to encourage our children to know all sorts of things. Knowledge possession makes people happy for many reasons.

-22-

PREPARING ASSIGNMENTS

"To be successful, the first thing to do is fall in love with your work."
Sister Mary Laureate

We will assume, for the purposes of this chapter, that you have chosen to work from textbooks similar to those your children would use in a public school. How do you know what they use and what you will subsequently have to look for? Think about the important classes you were required to take in High School. Core Curriculum includes:

> English
> Spelling
> Math
> Social Studies (Geography, History)
> Science/Health
> Physical Education
> Manuscript/Cursive study
> Reading/Literature

Additional Curriculum may include:

> Foreign Language Study
> Art and Art History
> Music
> Architecture History
> Home Economics
> Shop
> Auto Shop

To a Kindergarten curriculum, or for an older child that is not reading at grade level, make sure that you add a strong Phonics-Reading-Vocabulary program. It is possible that your non-reading older child has *never* been exposed to the complexities of the development of the English language. There are rules, and once learned, will teach them to 'sound out' anything. Don't steal your child's confidence by expecting him or her to go through life working only with sight words! (Sight words are the words that one knows intuitively, and generally, for a pre-schooler, start with the names of places your children are familiar with - "Target®", "McDonalds®", "Arby's®", "Kleenex®", and frequently used -"Walk", "Stop", etc.)

Don't mess around with curriculum or books you're not sure of on first glance. Trust your instincts to 'know' when what you have chosen will be suitable. Something will probably catch your eye if you're looking in the right place. If something doesn't jump out at you and appeal to you when you have taken a few minutes or more to look through and create a picture in your mind of your child and you working together through the book, chances are there is a reason why later on you might toss it aside then go in search of what you really wanted in the first place. It has happened with us on many occasions.

Curriculum purchases can be expensive, so play it safe. Explore as many possibilities as you can before purchasing. As I mentioned before, give this time, and allow yourself enough flexibility to back out of course work that it not suited to your child, or to you or your teaching style. If you are in a position of purchasing a curriculum that is built of small books, buy one or two at a time. Don't purchase a whole set, assuming that you can settle in with it. It may not be suited to you, your situation or your child. We have been burned on this, also. In reality, these decisions and mistakes were ours to make, and the curriculum suited other families just fine.

Work with your chosen curriculum for three or four weeks. Establish what is important and what is not. Start out with one good text for each subject, then determine what will allow you to spend about 20 to 30 minutes with that part of the curriculum each day. Remember this will vary by child, the child's age, and by text. If this seems short, remember that this is probably the actual course time the best public school teacher will be able to devote to this subject.

Think honestly about the amount of time the average teacher spends in the classroom. Of the six hours any teacher (even the best) can be in front of his or her children, only about three and a half to four hours can be devoted to core curriculum. Remember to subtract the time the teacher must spend disciplining and providing the time necessary to bring the slowest or the least cooperative of her students up to the level of the average student in the class. Performing the prescribed mathematics, we come back to a basic twenty to thirty minutes per subject per day. If, in fact, that subject is presented each and every day, which often does not happen.

In many schools, it is acceptable, on an elementary or intermediate level, to present, for example, Science once a week, or even once a month in a concentrated lab presentation. I do not personally feel this approach is adequate. There is just too much information available and necessary to learn.

While it is tempting to do so, I would not encourage a home schooling teacher to try to push a student into completing more than one 'assignment' per day. For example, if a text is set up for a first grader to complete two pages of math a day, do not stretch it to four or six pages, unless you are sure that the child has mastered the information completely before moving on. Also, remember that information is learned in each of the core subjects a bit at a time each day, so if you find that your child, for example, is having a good 'math' day, and you spend two hours on math, and you have allotted two and a half hours that day to home schooling, you may be tempted to cram the rest of the curriculum into the last half hour; or worse yet, you may feel that you need to push that student for an additional two hours beyond what he or she is developmentally ready for. As a practice, if I overshoot, and spend too much time on one subject (especially with my youngest), I usually will skip one assignment, and plan on attempting to do one and a half assignments in the missed subject over a period of two days with that child. Whatever works.

To keep yourself and your children on task, I would suggest that you keep some sort of record. This is the reason I developed the children's assignment sheets (found on the following page). Page 112 exemplifies a working example of how I fill in the assignment sheet, which takes a nominal amount of time and serves to keep me organized. I fill out the assignment sheets for tomorrow as I grade today's work, unless I can accurately predict that child's performance for the day, in which case, I may make notations as much as three or four days in advance. But it will always surprise you what will trip a

ASSIGNMENTS

Name_____

Today's Date is_____A_____   **The Day is** _____B_____

Reading	Read Pgs **C**	Quest Bk Pg **D**	Wkbk Pg **E**	Correct **F**	X	Y
Social Studies	Read Pgs **G**	Quest Bk Pg **H**	Wkbk Pg **I**	Correct **F**	X	Y
Science/ Health	Read Pgs **J**	Quest Bk Pg	Wkbk Pg	Correct **F**	X	Y
Math	Read Pgs **K** Set No.	Problems Set **L** Pg	even/odd Pg **L**	Correct **F**	X	Y
Spelling	Do Pgs **M**	Write Pgs **N** x ea		Correct **F**	X	Y
English	Read Pgs **O**	Quest Bk Pg **P**	Wkbk Pg **Q**	Correct **F**	X	Y
Foreign Lang.	Read Pgs **R**			Correct **F**	X	Y
Other Fun Stuff	**S**			**F**	X	Y
Phys. Ed	**T**					
Enrich.	**U**					
Other	**V**					

Vocabulary: 5x Each 1._____ 2._____

3. _____ 4._____W_____ 5._____

Look up and write 5x 1._____ 2._____

3._____ 4._____ 5._____

child and require additional practice or enrichment materials, so don't get too far ahead of yourself.

I have reproduced an example of the Assignment Sheet I am currently using on page 107.

A   It is best to reserve a place at the top of each assignment sheet for the date. This will serve as a record for you, and for anyone looking over your shoulder. It will also keep track of what was done when - knowing the date the work was completed will help you in a variety of ways.

B   In this space, I enter the day of the week. In the event that it appears that we have skipped a day of study, we will know what day it was, and I have also discovered that through the week, the children develop a certain pattern of behavior. For example, the first assignments performed on a Monday, often seem to be the lowest scores of the week. Those performed later on the same day, tend to be almost completely accurate. Also, since the children and I are almost always at home, it is easy to lose track of the days of the week. It also keeps us from working Saturdays!

C   This is the space I use when I am assigning page to page reading in the Literature textbook. Were I to change the textbook on this date, I would also the name of the new textbook in this space, then cross reference that back to the Cumulative Record.

D   This is the space I use to assign questions which mark the end of a Reading/Literature segment. These questions are important to determine reading comprehension.

E   This is where I would assign either Reading Workbook Assignments or related enrichment activities.

F   These are the columnar spaces I would have filled in to assign the necessary corrections from yesterday's work.

G   This is the space I use to indicate Textbook change, or a Social Studies reading assignment.

H   This is the space I utilize to assign questions which mark the end of a Social Studies daily Segment. Again, determination of comprehension is important.

I   This is the space I would use to assign Social Studies workbook Assignments or related enrichment activities.

J   This is the space I would utilize for Textbook changes, and Science reading assignment. The other spaces horizontally are used similarly to those for Reading and Social Studies.

K   We have, in the past, utilized a Saxon Math format, which has "Sets", or numbered lessons, followed by Alphabetical exercises connected to the reading, then problems numbered 1-30 for review. In this space, I indicate the Set No. and the Page Number. (Of course, for a standard Math text, I indicate the page numbers for the Math reading assignment).

L   These spaces are to indicate the locations and assigned problems indicated by Alphabetical and Numeric sequencing related to the Saxon Textbook. With a standard Math text, I would indicate numeric sequencing of the Exercises and odd, even, or all, or a Workbook Assignment.

M   This space indicates the pages of the consumable Spelling book to be completed. Since we are on a schedule which provides that the children complete two pages one day, followed by writing the words provided five times each the next, this space will only be filled on those days when assignments in the book are required.

N   This space indicates which page, and the number of repetitions required for the repetitive spelling word exercise. Repetitions of the correct spelling of these words builds vocabulary and provides a list of sight words to build upon, as well as phonetic sequencing useful in 'sounding out' words encountered otherwise in the curriculum or through outside reading. Repetitions also seat the words in the child's mind and triggers the 'it looks wrong' mechanism we all develop through experience.

O   This space indicates any name change for alternate or new English books. Because some concepts in grammatical usage are confusing, we use several different textbooks from time to time. We will place the page numbers of the pages to be read in this space, together with the name of the text.

P   This space indicates the questions and page numbers of the exercises to be completed from the English textbook.

Q   If we choose to use a workbook for enrichment on a subject in English usage, we indicate the name of the workbook, and page number here.

R   This is where we record the name of the Textbook for foreign language study, the pages to be written, and horizontally to the right, the problems to be worked, questions to be answered, or workbook questions to be completed.

      S   **Other Fun Stuff**, for us is a mishmash of all sorts of things. I use these three horizontal squares to limit myself to assigning only three elective-type additions per child. It is easy to overwork the kids, and if I only have three squares available for assignments, this serves as a reminder that they (and I) are not super-human. In the past, we have assigned Architecture, Art, Music, Math Enrichment, Mad Minutes, Sewing, Typing, and a variety of other lessons in these spaces. It is wise to limit yourself because there is a plethora of information out there that you can try to cram into your kids all at one time. Have patience and don't assign too much. Hopefully that material will still be fresh in your mind after you have completed the elective curriculum you already have in place. Or you can make a wish list. Also, you might (and if you are very coordinated and can do three or four things simultaneously) consider incorporating several elective subjects on different days of the week. High Schools and colleges do it, and there is nothing wrong with it, unless it becomes a confusing mess. For the first few months of home school, though, I would advise against making your work more complicated than it has to be.

      T   I pay attention to what my kids are doing outdoors. Usually, during the months of April through October, they swim a tremendous amount. Swimming for two hours at a time gives them plenty of exercise, fresh air, sunshine, and play time. In addition, we rollerblade with our kids, play basketball, soccer and baseball, ride bikes, hike, and---you name it. I write down what we do here in this space. If we do two or three things, I write those things down, too. I don't think going to the mall counts, but many people walk around malls with an exercise mindset. If you send the kids to the mall, please go with them! Unsupervised kids get kidnapped and sometimes get dragged into things you can't get them out of.

      Physical Education can be stretched to include just about anything, but be reasonable and use common sense. Make sure that your kids get out and move around every day. Also, check with your local authorities and determine whether it is *necessary* legally, for you to enroll your child in an organized physical education curriculum.

      U   Enrichment activities are mostly descriptions of Field Trips, though sometimes, they are indicative of lab days (dissecting earthworms or creating a wave tank).

V   **Other** is just that. Anything that I can't categorize any other way. Sometimes it happens and I have a space for it! How do you account for building a fountain or planting a garden, studying political candidates or perusing plant nurseries? Other.

W   **Vocabulary** - I fill in these spaces as I grade everything else. As I come across a misspelled word anywhere in the curriculum, I spell it correctly on the numbered lines. Our oldest son went from continuously having lists of 30 to 45 words to having 2 to 7 words per day. These are words that are spelled incorrectly, but used properly. If the child spells the word wrong five times, I insist that in addition to correcting the work from the day before, that the word be written properly five additional times the next day. Once a word is written on paper, it runs the risk of being engraved in stone in the child's mind. Requiring the additional writing may insure that the misspelling may never happen again. The Vocabulary section, at least in our school, is graded by the accuracy of the repetitions required. The children are always graded according to their course work, but the Grade, for example, in Reading, is never based upon spelling, except for absolutely beautifully perfect papers. An A+ is indicative of a paper which has been returned perfectly correct, with no spelling errors and nothing that needs correcting the next day. An A is given for a paper with a 90% or greater score, which may contain some spelling errors. Other than adding a + to an A, spelling does not play a role in whether or not a child has a change in a letter grade. On an A paper, a child can, (and has in the past) have as many as fifteen words spelled wrong and still have an A. This way, it is not discouraging for the child to see that while he has answered all the questions right, that his spelling has messed him up. The following day, that child can have an A+ in vocabulary if each of the fifteen words has had the proper five repetitions all spelled correctly. If the words on the vocabulary repetitions are spelled incorrectly, the grade for vocabulary reflects what is there and what is missing. Cursive and manuscript practice with the Vocabulary words are also included in the vocabulary grade for the day. If I can't read a word, it is wrong.

Look these up and write 5x - These spaces are for words that are either spelled incorrectly and used improperly, or spelled correctly and used improperly. *Their* and *there* end up here a lot, just like the mysterious *alot* word ends up here often. Sometimes I use these

Susanne L. Bain

ASSIGNMENTS

Name_____

Today's Date is 8-21-95   **The Day is** Monday

Reading	Read Pgs 178-181	Quest 1-4 Bk Act A,B Pg 179	Wkbk Pg 13,14	Correct WKBK Pg 11	✔	A
Social Studies	Read Pgs 19-23	Quest 1-5 Bk Pg 23	Wkbk Pg 1,2	Correct Pg 18-#3	✔	A+
Science/ Health	Read Pgs 109	Quest 1-10 Bk 1-10 Pg 109-110	Wkbk Pg	Correct —	✔	B
Math	Read Pgs 30-32 Set No.	Problems Set Pg	even/odd Pg 1-35 32	Correct pg 29 #18,20	✔	A-
Spelling	Do Pgs 30-31	Write Pgs x ea		Correct —	✔	A+
English	Read Pgs 87-88	Quest 1-10 Bk Pg 88-89	Wkbk Pg 32	Correct —	✔	B+
Foreign Lang.	Read Sp. Pgs 23	A-11 24		Correct —	✔	A
Other Fun Stuff	MAD MIN 133 A+	Am8 Pg34 A-	Architect Pg34-39 A	MAD MIN 132 Hm8 pg 33	✔✔	A+ A- A
Phys. Ed	Swimming 1.5hr	Basketbl .5hr			✔	A
Enrich.						
Other						

Vocabulary: 5x Each 1. pedestal   2. disappearing

3. boundaries   4. insufficient   5. Sabroso (Spanish)

Look up and write 5x 1. inertia   2. newton

3. their   4. there   5._____

spaces to prove a point about homophones, but these are necessary less and less often.

    X   This column of spaces (vertically) is used by *the kids* to make a check mark when they have finished all of their work in the horizontal line to the left. A reminder of progress!

    Y   This is the column that I use (vertically) to record the grade of everything to the left horizontally. I use a strict percentage for each assignment as I grade it, then give an average grade per day for each subject. I generally note a test with a circled letter grade so that when I look back at the sheet, it is easy to record on the cumulative grade sheet. This work takes approximately 30 to 60 seconds additionally in grading time per subject using my calculator. Please note that these grades are given before corrections are made, and are not changed. If I notice someone is slipping behind, we work on enrichment projects. Grading on a strict percentage means (to me)

$$90 - 100\% \rightarrow A$$
$$80 - 89\% \rightarrow B$$
$$70 - 79\% \rightarrow C$$
$$60 - 69\% \rightarrow D$$
$$59\% \searrow \quad \rightarrow F$$

If I make a mistake in grading, discover that the teacher's manual was wrong, or my calculations are wrong, I tell the child the moment I discover the mistake, and explain how it happened. It is only fair to let a child know when I make mistakes, and it also teaches your child how to handle a situation in which a mistake is made later as an adult, or how to handle a situation as an adult. I have also discovered many mistakes in teacher's manuals - especially in Math. If, for example, your child has a perfect paper, and one problem seems to be wrong time after time, it is possible that the child has the problem correct, and the teacher's edition has a misprint. This happens because human beings write books and textbooks are very complicated works. If in doubt, calculate the problem for yourself, or look up the answer and prove that your child is right.

-28-

CUMULATIVE GRADING

"Knowledge is of two kinds; we know a subject ourselves, or we know where can find information upon it."
Samuel Johnson

After entering grades as indicated, and as described above, I will then enter the grades to the Cumulative Grades Form (page 115), which is relatively self-explanatory. My goal here is to record the grades as simply and accurately as possible. Each of the textbook subjects is listed by category, leaving space for Enrichment and Additional Practice activities to occupy a second line so that I can more closely follow each child's progress in these subjects.

A   Make sure that if you have more than one child that anything that could conceivably used as a record and may be loose somewhere has that particular child's name on it. Twenty years from now, when he enters graduate school, this may be important. But then, maybe not. Who knows? But, for the moment, we can assume that records such as these may be important at some point in the future. Why not keep a record?

B   Remember that the sheet that I have shown here can be indicative of only fifteen days of work. Your child will be completing work at least for a period of several months, and perhaps for many years. If you loose leaf punch these grading sheets and stick them in a three pronged notebook, it will serve as a permanent record for you, and you may be able to save K-12 in the same notebook without ever purchasing a new one, and just by adding sheets, especially if you can find a big fat notebook. Number your sheets in case the notebook

Year___O___

CUMULATIVE GRADES

Sheet No___B___

Name___A___ **Days Att___C___**

Date:	D	D																		
Subject/Textbook																				
Reading	E																			
Spelling																				
Q																				
English																				
Math																				
Social Studies																				
Science																				
Foreign Language F																				
Enrichment																				
G																				
Field Trip/Dest. H	J K																			
Lab I	L M																			
Phys Ed. N																				
Typing																				
Vocabulary																				
P																				

flies open and the papers fall on the floor and you have to pick them up and put them in order!

C   Even though you have a record form that indicates 15 days worth of activity, that doesn't necessarily mean you will wish to fill in all the columns. For example, there are times when I leave a blank space and draw a line through it to indicate that we took a two week vacation for the holidays, then make a notation in Section **P** below of where we went and what we did. All of this could be classified as education, but there is no way to grade it. Leaving a columnar space or two will help you to identify what dates you were gone, and act as a signal later on when you need that information for some reason.

D   This is where you will record the dates (mo/day-- 12/15) horizontally across the top of your page. I would advise that you fill in these squares as you are recording the cumulative grades as indicated in **C** above in case you wish to leave columnar spaces empty for whatever reason. Again, here it is best not to get ahead of yourself, so you do not cause yourself confusion later.

E   These are the spaces where you will record your cumulative grades as transferred from column **Y** on the assignment sheets. Record one Reading Grade, one Math Grade, and so on. An alternative to using letter grades, of course, is recording the actual percentage your child achieved, then later coming back to average the percentages to come up with a more accurate assessment of your child's performance. Remember, I am not big on grading, only on learning. Many of us, though (and understandably so) feel strongly about record keeping and maintaining accurate grade records, and the percentage format would be much more informative or necessary. Remember, too, that the only reason you complete the cumulative grade sheet is to save you time when you later go back and figure out where your kids are going and where they are coming from and to access information which indicates to you how they are reacting to their texts and their environment. Scanning a sheet with a bunch of grades on it is better than plowing through individual sheets marked up with assignments at a time when you may be in a hurry and looking for something specific. In addition, Universities and Colleges will wish to see some sort of definitive scoring.

F   In this Foreign Language space, you may wish to record which language is being taught. Since we are using many

Foreign Language consumables, and will be switching to other languages in the future, we will need to know which language is being studied for this period of coursework. This is only necessary if you feel comfortable with and choose to teach a Foreign Language. Many well-rounded individuals survive their entire lives without knowing another language and lead full and productive lives. It is not mandatory! Remember, though, that some Universities are requiring two years of a foreign language before admission. Check with the University or college of your choice before making a decision.

G   I have left myself two spaces here to write down the actual names of the Enrichment materials I have chosen to use. Again, leaving two spaces reminds me that I have to go to extra work to record grades for the kids. This reminds me that we are not super-human and cannot handle more than what is already on the plate in front of us. If I have to skip down below the Vocabulary section on the sheet to record the name of a book and the grades, it is a caution to myself to slow down and be more reasonable. Keep in mind that because of the nature of Enrichment, there may be as few as two or three grades for Enrichment materials, and when reviewing the grades in this section, the titles of the books may change in mid week depending on the amount of additional material necessary. Keep in mind that this is only a record and not an instruction book.

H   As a rule, our family usually takes one field trip per two or three weeks. Sometimes it is more, and sometimes it is less. We do what we have time for and according to interests and requirements of the studies the children perform. There is space in this slot for the destination and space down below in area **P** to note additional information or additional field trips.

I   Again, as a rule, we generally only have one or two lab days per fifteen teaching days. This space gives us room to write one activity down, with additional space in area **P** to cross reference additional activities.

J/K   In this section I cross reference any field trip in area **P** against the grade information I would give during a Field Trip. For example, the listing for a field trip cross referenced as **2** in the **P** area, where the child's behavior was fine, we had a great time, and we learned a great deal would be 2/A+.

L/M   As in section **J/K**, I would cross reference in this area any Lab work that we had performed and noted in area **P** against the grade information we would have for the lab performed. For example, a listing for a laboratory on dissecting an earthworm, referenced as **3** in the **P** area where the child had failed to find any of the organs because the dissection had been performed sloppily and not according to the lab notes provided, and where the child had answered 25% of the questions asked in the written section of the lab incorrectly, the notation would be 3/C- (depending on how annoyed I had become, and whether there was anything entered in the lab notebook!)

N   As a rule, I don't grade my kids on playing, but we do occasionally use a book to study the rules of team sports and occasionally, the kids don't exactly behave in sportsmanlike ways. In general, the grade in this space will be an A for lack of a better place holder unless something remarkable happens (A+) or something socially devastating happens (C). All of which to say, Physical Education is taught three of six days in our public schools here for 1/2 hour a day. Our kids in our home school must play together each day relatively quietly and perform fairly when they are playing, and when participating in a game with rules, they have to follow the rules. PE can be graded or not. We like to make sure our children stay healthy. Sunshine and fresh air helps out greatly in both categories.

O   The years will fly by quickly, and giving the month and the date for this year will mean nothing in six years. This is a nice space to record the year on each of the sheets - again if they are dropped it will be much easier to identify last year's work, and to identify when December stops and January starts.

P   As mentioned many times in the above text, the space below the grading grid can be important in recording important things that happened during this period of time.   If your child has experienced an extended (or even short) illness, extra field trips (explanation of activities and how the child responded), labs (whether or not the child responded positively, or whether the activity should be repeated at a later time). This is a good miscellaneous space to report all of the "other" activities as recorded on the assignment sheet. Anything that will help you later in remembering something peculiar, fascinating, or important can be reported here. Sometimes details will help later in determining where a problem showed up or where a big jump was made developmentally.

Q   Recording the name of your child's textbooks in these spaces is important because at some point you may wish to switch back and forth, change the textbook, or graduate to the next level. As you home school, and especially if you utilize our method, you will find that the kids will slip ahead in some books and encounter a great deal more work in others. Math and English books are set up for one lesson per day per public school day (approximately 8 months of M-F work.) Social Studies and Science, (especially on a below-fifth grade level) are planned for approximately one or two lessons per week. If you are working through your books with an assignment each day, your third grader may suddenly find him/herself in a fifth grade social studies book. If he or she is up to it, why not? I've given myself plenty of room here to record the name of the book and the grade level for future reference.

Year 94

CUMULATIVE GRADES

Sheet No 25

Name

DaysAtt 16

Date: June 1-16	1	2	3	4	5	7	8	9	0	1	2	3	4	5	6
Subject/Textbook															
Reading Focus - 8	B	A	A	A	A		A	A	A	B	A			A	B
Spelling A/W - 8	B	A	A	A	B		A	A	A	B	A			A	A
English McM - 8	C	A	A	A	B		A	B	A	D	B			A	B
Math Saxon/Holt - 9	D	S	D	B	D		B	A	D	T	A			A	A
Social Studies SB - 8	B	A	A	A	B		A	A	B	C	B			A	A
Science Mer rill - 9	C	A	B	B	A		A	B	B	C	A			B	A
Foreign Language Hayes	B	A	A	A	A		A	A	A	C	A			A	B
Enrichment Mad Min	B	A	A	A	A		A	A	A	A	B			A	A
Art History	C	A	B	A	A		A	A	A	B	A			A	A
Field Trip/Dest. Mesa Verde						A						1 A			
Lab D/S - Earthworm		A										2 A	2 A		
Phys Ed.	A	A	A	B	A		A	A	A	A	A			A	A
Typing															
Vocabulary	A	A	A	A	A		A	A	A	A	A			A	A
Math Enr - HM8											A			A	B
1-Phoenix Zoo F/T															
2-Electricity Exp-Circuits															
6/1 Cold/Fever															

-24 -

USING THE CUMULATIVE GRADE GRID FOR DIAGNOSTICS

"Character builds slowly, but it can be torn down with incredible swiftness."
Faith Baldwin

If, in examining the cumulative grading grid looking for a solution to one of the kid's problems, I spotted a row of grades that seem to be slipping, it would be easy to identify an area which might need more attention and perhaps additional practice. Depending upon the course work and test grades, we could determine whether or not we need to change the textbook or merely slow progress down until we reach an acceptable equilibrium. Columnar slippage, exemplified by poor performance on one day followed by acceptable grades the next is usually indicative of some sort of day long distraction or perhaps just a tired child. Unless it is a pattern, I generally will not adjust curriculum, but require the corrections, as usual, to be completed the next day. I have provided a suggested usage of the Cumulative Grades form for a few weeks in June. While this set of grades is indicative of something we experienced with one of our children, it is by no means a representation of grades and the like that occur frequently, but a representation of how this grid might be used.

As you will look at the sample, you will note that in the left hand column, I have noted initials I can later decode for the names and the grade levels of the textbooks I am using. We can look across the grid and very quickly tell quite a few things about this sixteen day period.

121

✔Notice that 6/6 is not listed because I felt there was no academic activity worth reporting, but I did report 6/7, as we participated in a field trip to Mesa Verde. (An Archeological Site).

✔The weekend of the 3rd and 4th, the children went to the Zoo and participated in Electricity Experiments on Circuitry. These are the sorts of things that I feel are worth noting.

✔Note that on 6/4, this particular child seemed to have some sort of problem in sportsmanship which necessitated a drop in his A average to a grade of B for the day. Something must have occurred while the children were playing basketball, soccer, or swimming. If I look up that particular day in the assignment sheets, I will find an explanation for the B which I didn't feel was worthwhile to burden the cumulative grade report with.

✔Note that the Earthworm dissection went well (a notation that means that the child was ready for the responsibility of dissection and will be able to tackle the frog in a few weeks when we again have the time to do it.)

✔The Electricity Experiments were a whopping success. For a two day group of experiments, the children worked well together, and were relatively unsupervised. This child led discussion, and provided additional instruction for his siblings. Reports were turned in and questions were answered properly with no spelling errors. This was an enjoyable experiment and indicates to me the following

a.   The children were ready for the work developmentally.
b.   The product was useful and was age appropriate. We will continue to purchase lab materials and sets from this manufacturer because nothing was missing and everything worked properly.
c.   This child was ready for the responsibility of leading a team effort in a subject he knew relatively little about.
d.   While this experiment could have been a below-grade-level experience for this particular child, the knowledge gained was knowledge he had not studied in the past, and he handled himself very well. He was able to answer questions for his siblings. Any problems that he could not apply himself to readily were looked up elsewhere.

   *   A note on this particular experiment. It was an excellent short course in circuitry with all equipment included in the set. A videotape as well as instructional written material were included for the

construction of the several experiments to be performed. There are many such kits, and the ones we have found seem quite appropriate, fun and quite an entertaining way to introduce scientific subjects as an alternative to diagramming and reading textbooks. It has become apparent to me that it is nice to go and purchase pre-packaged laboratory experiments, because you don't need to purchase more of anything than you absolutely require for the project. The down side of this practice is that the sets can be expensive. The up side is that many include video tapes which seem to interest the children and keep their attention in a witty and positive way.

✔If you will note the column (6/1) indicated by the **1**, you can follow the grid vertically and find that the grades are not necessarily indicative of the child's other performance on the grid. For example, this child normally scores A's in Reading, Spelling, English, and other subjects with the exception of Math. On this day, the Math grade was particularly bad. It was during this day that we re-evaluated this child's situation, and decided that the possibility of field trips or labs might relieve a little tedium for him. Another possibility to consider would be the order in which the work was performed, and the fact that is was a Monday. There is a possibility that this child may have been ill on this day. Down at the bottom of the page, we note, however, that on 6/1 this child had a cold. The following day, most of the grades were back up again, and we stopped worrying, though we continued to monitor his Math and his health very closely.

✔In column (6/11), **2,** we see that the grades once again dropped. With no evidence of illness, we again assess his progress, and see that the grade that stands out is an F in Math. At that point, we sat down with the child and talked to him about his performance in Math. As I have mentioned elsewhere in the book, this child seemed to have an ongoing frustration with the Saxon Math program (note, however that I know many families using it successfully. It depends totally on the child). It was during this discussion, that we decided to pull this child out of the Saxon Grade 8 program and put him in a 9th Grade Pre-Algebra program. As you can see by the grades in the row indicated by the number **3**, his grades improved. There are a few things to watch with this child in later months.

*The first several grades in a new book are, again, indicative of review tasks which may not ensure the appropriateness of the new textbook.

*If a child is doing poorly in a book just to get rid of it, it may be a sign that the child is attempting to take control of his own study. (Which may not be all bad, but could be a sign of manipulation). We are not sure what it was about the format of the Saxon book this child did not like, but part of the agreement is indicated in the row marked **4**.

✔Note in the row marked **4** that an additional HM8 book was added. This is an additional enrichment-practice book which was added as part of the agreement to switch to the new Algebra book. Because this child had not yet completed a prescribed 8th grade course work in Math (which may or may not have been a problem in entering Algebra), we felt that it was necessary to continue the type of rudimentary mathematics it might take to get him through upper level math. So we have supplied him with a small enrichment workbook that he has agreed to complete simultaneously with the Algebra that would give him that additional practice.

If it all seems complicated, remember that these are a rough description of experiences which occurred over a period of two and a half weeks, and which generated much discussion and concern. What I have hoped to describe here is how a decision was made to determine the appropriateness of learning materials, weighing the psychological impact of the change in curriculum against the child's ability to adjust properly and not pull control of the curriculum too much out of our hands. In addition, my hope is to have created somewhat of a picture of what can be achieved by record keeping which may seem rigid, somewhat inflexible, unnecessary, or rather stifling. Granted, it takes a few minutes each day to fill out the extra form, but it may be worth the time if you fail to notice a problem which might otherwise be glaring at you. You might avert the stress you feel at watching your child flail around for weeks or months, and give you the extra information you will need to make an important decision for your child.

In addition, we have since discovered that college admissions personnel require such documentation when considering a home schooled student for admission.

-25 -

ORDER OF OPERATIONS

"One must pass through the circumference of time before arriving at the center of opportunity. "

Baltasar Gracian

I would never presume to say that the Assignment sheet is the commission of the order in which the children are suppose to work through their books each day. I make only two requests of my children. They must complete at least what I assign. And they have to do Math and English (either order) first. Math and English seem to require the most day to day actual new learning of anything else I present to the kids. With the possible exception of the problems experienced early Mondays, the kids are freshest first thing in the morning, provided they have had a high-protein breakfast. (Did you know we all do better when we limit our sugar intake, especially in the morning???? Eat a teaspoon or two of sugar on an empty stomach and wait a half hour. Do you feel tired? Most kids do.)

Allowing the children to take the initiative to plan out their day and complete all their assignments in the order they choose creates a sense of trust and fulfillment in that they feel I have faith in their abilities in planning and completion. I frankly don't care in which order I grade their work, but I feel most relieved when the really knowledge intensive stuff is complete, because there seems to be a certain amount of stress involved in learning entirely new and intense material. Why not get it out of the way first?

125

The order of the assignment sheet is, then, perfectly arbitrary, and just something I've worked out to fit the time and the place on the day I worked it out on the computer. In essence, I've placed basic skills first, followed by enrichment and electives. On days when we slow down - for example, through the summer or on vacation, the basic skills and core subjects are at the top of the page and filled in, while the electives may not have an entry for a few weeks.

Your child will probably choose to do his favorite assignment first, or leave it for the last subject of the day. Why not let him decide and be flexible with him. In a world where children will later need to make big decisions, starting with the small ones at a young age will encourage a certain amount of creativity. Remember, also that moving along faster in a book than prescribed is not *cheating,* nor is it *wrong.* It is merely accelerated advancement. In a private school it would be considered self-guided accelerated learning. This is what some home schooling families strive for and cherish.

Later, your child will encouter situations in college where he will need to make value judgments about assignments which must be performed in seemingly short periods of time without adequate time to complete everything. Providing early guidance for your child in time-management will later help him to make the informed decisions he will need to make both in college and professional life which will help him to excel while others may founder because these decisions were made for them by teachers. In addition, an attitude of learning will later help these students to view their work as exercises rather than punishment and knowledge-growth rather than senseless drill.

-*26*-

TOOLS/SCHOOL SUPPLIES

"Love: An ocean of emotions entirely surrounded by expenses."
Thomas R. Dewar

As I write this, it is *Back to School* time, and I can read the ads and chuckle, because our back to school time is all year round. The neat thing about *Back to School* time for the kids in public and private schools is that it is almost like the holiday season when moms and kids are all scurrying around the Kmart® looking for good stuff to spend money on. Some of the money is well spent, and, well, quite frankly, some isn't. In the broadest sense, *Back to School* sales can mean a reduction in home school costs for us in any event.

Home schooling can be done on an as-needed basis, and I have seen many permutations of what we are doing. Honestly speaking, the way my family does things is rather cumbersome, but it works for me and the kids because everything is organized, separated and each subject stands alone.

✔We use **one 120 page spiral notebook for each subject** from fourth grade through twelfth grade. This means that we bought lots of notebooks at the onset. I buy them in six-packs at the local warehouse store which reduces this burden quite effectively.

At this point you may think that because 120 page spiral notebooks have three sections - ha! One notebook can serve for three subjects! Nope. We tried that. It didn't work, because many times we use five pages per math assignment, to only one page for English, and sometimes two pages for Science. Pretty soon, we had the equivalent of one notebook per subject anyway, and the lessons were very hard for me to find, and the notebooks get rather scraggly and ill-

127

used looking.

Using one spiral notebook per subject also provides an excellent record for your child. All math from past assignments is readily available while the child is doing today's math assignment. Likewise, past English assignments act as a reference for current work. As teacher, I can easily compare past experiences *per subject,* looking for trends, problems, strengths and weaknesses then provide remedial or accellerated work as needed without the distraction and confusion of the other subject assignments.

✔You can make your labels for the kids' spiral notebooks using **sticky backed address labels** (the white ones that are about 3 and a half inches long and about an inch and a half wide that come in a roll at an office supply store.) I tear them in half, then fold them over so that they stick out about a half an inch or so from the right side of the notebook (like a notebook tab) and write the name of the subject on each side, so that you can read them whether the notebook is upside down or right side up. I do this because I haven't found an ink yet that will stick to the shiny coating they use for the covers of the spital notebooks. Also, somewhere on this label, I write the child's initial and the grade level). Figure you will use **about two spiral notebooks per subject per year per child** for subjects that require writing (non-consumable textbooks) and for spelling. Remember, that right now, all you will need to buy is one notebook per subject per child to match the number of hardcover textbooks each child will use, **plus one for Spelling and another for Vocabulary.**

✔**I would advise you not to use loose leaf notebook paper** unless you are making some sort of submittal to a contest or something outside of your own use, and never, never tear out the sheets of the spiral notebooks because that is messy, unsightly, becomes very disorganized, and easy to lose. Remember, your child's work won't get turned in to a teacher in a stack with thirty other papers, and it is nice to have everything organized and in its own place. Also, the kids don't get into the habit of folding their assignment in half inside of a book which is a practice that college professors despise.

✔Make sure that your children have a good supply of **number two pencils.** As an alternative, your child might try a mechanical pencil. Don't let them drop the lead inserts from the mechanical pencils on the floor and step on them. Also, stock up on eraser inserts, which can be purchased separately, usually at the same place you purchase the pencils. If you use traditional pencils, you are probably best off with an electrical pencil sharpener. It saves a lot of mess.

✔Use a **colored pen or pencil** that you feel comfortable with and that you find doesn't give you writer's cramp. I use a red razor point marker or a ball point. This will encourage you, as the teacher, to give your children the kind of positive feedback they will need in order to perform their corrections properly. I keep about six red pens in my box with my stickers. This gives me the flexibility to move around and leave them all over the house as I work with each of the kids. Also, having a bunch of pens around helps in case someone swipes one to color red when they can't find their red crayon. I still have something to grade with until I find the missing one.

✔Remember to grade your child's work in a color different from your child's work so that he or she can easily identify your comments and get on with corrections without bothering with those problems she has already learned to solve or material he has already mastered.

✔**If you have more than one child**, and you fully intend to work with your children in years to come, and you encounter workbooks that you like a lot and that go with your hard backed textbooks....**don't let your first child fill in the workpages.** If the workbook indicates somewhere on the cover that the sheets are reproducibles, reproduce a set for your oldest child, and use a three ring notebook to keep it all together. Do this before you are even tempted to make an assignment in the only copy you have in this book, otherwise, you will have to manually reproduce the worksheet, or, even messier, white out or erase the work the first child does. (You won't want to do this more than once, because it is tedious and it wastes time.) Yes, I do use three ring notebooks, but not for loose leaf paper - I use them for reproduced copies of workbooks. None of the work my children produce is loose. It all goes into some sort of a notebook for back reference.

✔**Be mindful of copyright laws and do not sell copies of your workbooks to other people! Also, it is unwise to copy workbooks or worksheets that are not marked "reproducible".** If the workbook is non-reproducible, have your child work the problems in a separate notebook as he would an assignment from a textbook.

✔Supply your upper grade children with **a nice pen**. This can be given as a gift for completion of a *manuscript* book and signal the start of the *cursive* curriculum. Remember the pens that leaked in your purse? Picture that mess on your kitchen table, or on your favorite chair. Don't deal with it. The cost of a box of cheap pens is about the same as a single nice one. You will go through a box of cheap pens, or one nice one and possibly two $.75 refills in a year or two (if that). Also, you can let your kids borrow the one you carry around in your purse. The first time they forget to give it back and you discover it is missing in the supermarket will be a reminder about borrowing and returning. They will need a pen, in any event, to work on their cursive and produce reports.

✔**I keep a 3" loose leaf notebook with insert page covers** (the vinyl ones that fill at the top) for special projects the kids come up with. Art projects, reports, thesis, poetry and special tests go in these 'permanent' notebooks, and the kids are very proud of them. This is what we show to grandma and grandpa and friends when they come to visit, and they are worth showing. If you can find them, the ones with the clear vinyl covers that you can slip a page into for a front cover work nicely. I display what the child considers to be his or her best art work as the front cover, then move it back into the vinyl protectors when he or she comes up with something better. This is totally optional, and, of course, not necessary. It is a nice touch I do for my kids.

✔My mother gave me a special gift in a decorated box that is a little wider than a 3x5 card that works perfectly for my sticker collection. It is fun picking out **stickers** to match the kids moods, the holidays and the changing of the seasons. Many of the stickers I have found have the name of extinct or endangered animals on them. I have found foreign language stickers which use the vocabulary I am teaching in reassuring comments; as well as science, social studies, and birthday themes. If you pay attention, there is no limit to what is being printed on stickers these days. As I mention elsewhere, I prefer the stickers that are pre-glued, which are easily transferred and come in small sheets of a dozen or so. Small ones about an inch square are perfect for almost everything. Large ones (I have found some five inch dinosaurs) are wonderful when someone gets a really fabulous grade on a subject struggled with. Again, the idea of using **stickers** to **indicate work completed** is just an idea of mine that works for me. It makes it easier for me to leaf through a notebook or binder and find the page I need to be on, and clues me in on corrections that have been neglected if there is no sticker on the page.

✔For younger students - K-2, find **pre-lined manuscript paper**. I doubt that the percentage of 5-7 year olds capable of writing legibly on college ruled spiral paper is very high. This I triple punched and inserted in a 2" binder and used for spelling tests and manuscript practice. Because the repetition in the lower level spelling books is so high, and the number of words presented per chapter is relatively low, I found that even without the five repetitions, my youngest still scored almost complete 100% on spelling tests after four days of working with the words. Some children may need the extra practice. As he advanced into the third grade level book, the five repetitions became necessary; and he was ready for college ruled spiral bound paper.

✔There is a need, also, for **2-pocket lightweight portfolios with clips** to accommodate **sundry enrichment programs,** as well as keeping **assignment sheets** together. As a matter of practice, I use bright pink pocket binders for assignment sheets (which I punch holes in and insert in the center binder section - don't use the pockets for assignment sheets, because they will get lost, stepped on and destroyed and you want to keep those), printing the kid's names visibly on the outside of the notebook. I pre-punch and put 30 assignment sheets in each, and these last approximately six weeks. These assignment sheets create a permanent record that can be kept and stored for future reference. We store the few loose assignments for that period of time in the pockets (graphs, maps, etc.).

Other notebooks are useful for long term projects, reports, photocopied reproducible thematic units (we had, for example, units on time and money that we used this for, and, at one time a unit on Architecture) and the like. At any given time I usually have five or six of these floating around between the three kids for various reasons. Use the clips to maintain the integrity of the material that is important to keep, and pockets for loose things like scratch paper that you have no intention of keeping once the notebook is filed away in storage.

✔**Two reams of the paper** which works well in your printer are a definite necessity if you intend to use your computer for home schooling. Remember that not all paper is suitable for all printers. If you find something that works, buy enough to last awhile, and you will thank yourself in the long run if your supplier runs out of your favorite brand when you have run out. It happened to us.

✔**A three hole punch** is a necessary thing to have if you anticipate making or reproducing worksheets, assignment sheets, cumulative grade reports or anything else for your children. These are available at your local office supply warehouse store, and I have also seen them at membership warehouses.

✔An office **stapler** for your use and for the use of your children. The ones that cost just a touch more don't jamb as often. Buy **extra staples** at the time you purchase your stapler so you are sure to have the correct type on hand.

✔A quality pair of sharp **scissors** you don't mind using on paper comes in handy. Also a pair of **children's safety scissors** should be purchased for a child K-2.

✔For K-2, a box of **ten primary/secondary crayons** for teaching, and a **larger box** with more colors for other purposes.

✔**Watercolor markers** work well for map work through high school. The older the child, the nicer the pens, because older children tend to replace caps.

✔A box of big fat **sidewalk chalk** is nice to have around for drawing scale models of elephants and whales on the driveway in front of your house (as well as drawing hopscotch squares).

✔Because we use so many different notebooks, it is nice to be able to flip to the pages to be graded or corrected quickly. I handle locating these pages by placing a sticky note at the top of each page to be corrected. It hangs out of the top of the notebook like a flag, and enables me to skip all the pre-corrected material and get to work quickly. I find the smallest **Post-It Notes™ (1"x1")** for these flags, then use the larger ones **3"x3"** for additional notes inside the books. I use the lined ones to give additional directions or to assign questions that may not appear in the book and that I feel are important to the curriculum. While this may seem an expensive answer to a relatively simplistic problem, remember that your time is worth something. Also, since the notes can be removed and reused, we find that they are around, sometimes, for a few weeks until the sticky is all gone and they go into the recycling bin or are used for telephone messages and later discarded.

While there are all sorts of products offered for use by home schoolers and teachers, it is your job to protect your finances and stick to your own budget. We forego such things as posters in favor of notebooks, paper and enrichment materials. We look closely at book clubs to make sure there are no semi-permanent strings that need to be cut if we no longer wish to be a part of it. Also, we carefully weigh the probability of needing items offered in bulk for a seemingly better price when a smaller amount would do just as well. Consider splitting a box of something here and there with other parents or home schoolers in the area (such as cases of paper, three ring notebooks, binders and spiral notebooks) and sharing the discount. You will probably not find bargains at teacher's supply stores, but you may find things you will not find elsewhere. Be creative in your thinking, and remember that everything I've mentioned above can either be purchased at a discount warehouse supply or an office supply warehouse. You may also already have most of these items, and need merely to reassess how you use them. Membership fees at warehouse store are almost always saved on the first trip, and many supplies used in home schools can be used for multi-purpose.

Also, consider looking into discount catalogs, such as Oriental Trading Company® (address in the Index at the back of the book). While you may need to buy in bulk and store what you don't need immediately, the discounts offered may be worth your effort in sorting through the products and finding what you need at a slightly (or greatly) better price. When I first started home schooling, I began using shiny stickers to mark pages already graded. I have done that through grade 12, and it is still fun to find appropriate, funny, or seasonal stickers to mark pages with. It would surprise you how much faster grading can be if you and your child don't have to hunt down corrections and new assignments.

-27-

The Home Schooling List of Necessary (And Not so Necessary) SUPPLIES

"To need nothing is divine, and the less a man needs the nearer does he approach to divinity."

Socrates

Socrates was lucky. He didn't have to answer to the authorities about the education of his children at home, so he didn't have endless paperwork to complete, and supplies were cheaper in his time. In some ways, it was to his advantage that paper was almost nonexistent. Here's a quick review of Chapter 26 in shorthand form.

1.   **One** 120 page **spiral notebook per hardbound text** (or core subject) **plus Spelling and Vocabulary per student.**
2.   At least **one loose leaf binder w/dividers** per child
          and/or
     One 1" notebook per subject per reproduced workbook
3.   **A box of #2 pencils** (Start with 6-10 per child)
          or
     One Mechanical Pencil w/extra leads and erasers per child.
4.   Two (or several) **red pens** for grading.
5.   **One nice pen per child** after third grade. (Unless you are willing to share and risk losing yours).

6. (Optional) **One 3" loose leaf binder** w/a vinyl insert to slip artwork into per child.
7. (Optional) One box of vinyl top loading **page protectors** (pre-punched for 3-ring binder).
8. (Optional) A collection of colorful grading **stickers** to get you started.
9. For K-2, **pre-lined manuscript paper** and a binder to keep it in.
10. A half dozen or so **2-pocket lightweight portfolios** w/3 clips ea (hopefully in assorted colors) for Assignment books and Enrichment projects.
11. A **three ring binder** in which to store cumulative grades - One for the family might be adequate. Be sure to use dividers.
12. Two reams of **typing** or computer **paper.**
13. (Optional) **3-Hole Punch.**
14. **Stapler** and staples.
15. **Scissors** for cutting paper. Make sure you have a pair for yourself, and a pair of safety scissors if you are dealing with anyone younger than 8.
16. For K-1 - One Box of **10 crayons** (Red, Green, Blue, Black, Purple, Yellow,...etc.)
17. For K-2 - **Large box of crayons** with exotic names (See Using Crayons section)
18. (Optional) Sidewalk **Chalk.**
19. (Optional) A package of **Post-It-Notes©**
20. Don't forget the **textbooks!**

*There are probably other things, but this will at least get you started. Remember all these things don't have to be purchased new, and you may most everything around the house, or your kids may have them in their rooms. Remember, too, that these are just supplies. Finding Textbooks will probably be just a bit more challenging. Don't panic!

-*28* -

CONVENTIONS

"Luck is a matter of preparation meeting opportunity."
Oprah Winfrey

Remember that the assumption of individuals displaying tools and texts at conventions is that they will turn a profit on what they sell. We demand, they supply. We shared a wonderful afternoon with our children at our first home school convention and discovered a week later that children had been strictly forbidden on the display floor. Odd for home schoolers who stress absolute parenting! I can complain about this all I want, but unless someone else joins the chorus, I'm just one voice.

But, as I said, we made a great field trip out of the day and spent four hours looking through the materials available, and discovered that most of the display booths were manned by home schoolers utilizing products they were selling. These individuals, we found to be helpful, friendly, honestly interested, and extremely courteous. Two booths, in particular were manned by opportunistic professional salesmen who had the tact of Ferengi. Force feeding information (or even worse, textbooks) to a reticent new home schooling mother is like dangling a kitten in front of a rottweiler. I was put off by these individuals and the correspondence schools who hired these "suits" should be ashamed of themselves for condoning such tactics. Fortunately, in recent years many of these tactics have diminished so perhaps others will follow suit and become kinder and more tactful.

I was hoping, in attending the convention, to convince myself that home schooling parents are not, in general (these are all the myths I've seen in the papers)

⊗**Too lazy to get out of bed** and take their kids to school. Not true! Over 2000 parents had already visited the displays before 10:00 in the morning on a Friday. They had to be out of bed by at least 7:00 to do so!

⊗**Undereducated.** Not true! I found those in the crowd and behind the booths to be lucid, friendly, and in general, well dressed, well nourished, healthy intellectuals who could, as a group read at a high school level or above. (The average American reads at or below a 4th Grade Level).

⊗**Aging Hippies.** Of the transient group of two thousand or so we encountered we saw not one withering flower child. Quite the contrary, I suspect that most of those involved were college educated, stable individuals with a genuine interest in finding an alternative to drug and gang infested schools. In addition, we saw only one tattoo, and no outward evidence of substance abuse. Most home schooling parents, by the way, are quite conservative.

⊗**Running from Adversity.** I prefer to think that most home schoolers are opting for a laterally thought-out alternative that places them in a position to control their own futures and that of their children.

If you are vacillating on your decision to home school at all, you will find it interesting to attend a home schooling convention. If the one you attend is at all like the one we visited, you will find the displays fascinating, and the merchandise offered of outstanding value. Unfortunately, we did not have time to attend the seminars offered, however, we greatly appreciated and enjoyed the array of products offered, and the well-thought out assemblage of textbooks, enrichment programs, computer software, games, and laboratory equipment. Also, they displayed many companies representing everything from sticker and stamp manufacturers, to t-shirt shops specializing in educational/home school supplies, and a local music store which caters to home schoolers who offer instruments and music instruction to their children.   We also discovered, that like schools, we can subscribe to many periodicals at a discount for our children, which are very similar to some of the weekly newspaper-type periodicals the kids used to bring home from school.

We asked many questions, as did our children. We found the display personnel to be as helpful and patient with us as with our children. Even with the big crowd, and even though our children were not technically welcome, most of these people seemed pleased to have our time and interest.

I guess what impressed me the most was that in a showroom the size of a major airline hangar, we heard more people saying 'excuse me' and 'thank you' in four hours than we heard in an entire year at any of the public schools our children attended---either by teachers or students. For that matter, we heard more pleasant conversation than we have heard in the last five years in any local restaurant or other place of business. This was brought to my attention by my children who recognize that home schooling families are just plain different than average people.

In addition, we have received many catalogs, brochures and "Thank you" cards from the people we met. And we met many people.

Visiting such a convention may be a turning point in your opinion of the option of home schooling, and I hope that even if you have made the decision to place your children back into public or private school, that you will consider making a stop at the next convention in your area just to explore, listen, and learn.

The showroom floor is also an opportunity to open books offered by textbook manufacturers and planned curriculum representatives. As such, you may have an opportunity to look products over before you buy them. Since most conventions run the floor for two days, you can look the first day, then go back the second day and buy after you've slept on it. Many of the home schooling parents I know plan on attending the convention because they know that they will want to buy everything they need in the way of textbooks and enrichment programs for their children for the following year. I prefer to look at the textbooks and items offered, and take business cards and catalogs, so that I can peruse them at my leisure, then place orders. I'm sure either way is just as acceptable. But the hands on opportunity is one that shouldn't be missed.

-29-

USING BOOKS
Letting your Children's Textbooks Work for You

"Books have led some to learning and others to madness."

Petrarch

With a general idea of the type of books you wish to use, and having purchased what you feel to be the most adequate and appropriate of the available titles, you, as a parent can do one of many things, or a combination of any of them. You can start at the beginning and work to the end, which is what you will be, for all intents, forced to do, if you have purchased a prepared curriculum or working with an outside source, such as a staff of curriculum instructors at a correspondence school.

In using textbooks, as we do, we generally take the time to prepare some sort of diagnostic test to determine (especially in Math and English) where the children fall in the book from the standpoint of prior knowledge. Remember, that in the average school system, teachers are working with children who have taken three months off from their learning experiences, have forgotten much of what they learned during the last part of the year in anticipation of their summer vacation, and are generally not particularly motivated to learn for approximately six weeks at the beginning of any school year after first grade. Kindergarten and first grade are easy, and I'll get to that in a minute.

Generally speaking, the beauty of home schooling is that it need not stop for traditional vacations unless you wish to do so. If you have a child moping around the house with nothing to do, you can always assign him something, and send him off to a well-lit table or out into the yard, and start him on a learning adventure of some sort.

Because temper-atures in our part of the country soar to over 115 degrees, summer is not a fun time for children. So we home school throughout the year. When it is time for our children to skip up to the next grade level, especially in Math and English, we do some diagnostic testing. This is much easier than it sounds.

The Math and English textbooks we use provide End of Chapter Review pages which summarize the work that was to have been completed in the weeks preceding the test. We generally skip the pages before the first test and administer that first chapter test. Generally speaking, you can probably count on your child to forget something. Children are human. The information contained in the test, by definition, is found somewhere in the pages preceding it. If enough of the test is missed to require additional practice, go back in that chapter in the book, and assign that section or those sections that seem to give your child difficulty, then either readminister the same test (a marginally good idea) or come up with your own. That is when it is nice to have a word processor, because it really doesn't take much time once you have the formula in the form of the test your child just took to look at and create from. Make sure you familiarize yourself with the scope of the material covered before creating a test on your own so your child can be reasonably aware of the answers if he has studied and retained the information.

Once your child has shown you that he or she has mastered the first few sections (or maybe just the first one, depending on the publisher), press on, assigning one section per day. If the work seems easy or boring for your child, you might consider moving a little faster by assigning every second or every third problem in two sections at a time until you hit something they really need help with. That is the time you should slow down.

Relax. Its okay. Your child is now several weeks beyond the work that would have been performed at the same stage of development in a child who has had a gap in learning. Let him slow down and learn. This testing, by the way, takes little more than a few days at the beginning of each book. Remember that most textbooks are formula books. MacMillan® Language Arts, for example, utilizes the same basic knowledge in the same basic order in each successive year, but adds additional information as the children are ready for details to be added as the years progress.

Social studies and science textbooks roughly follow a similar format among publishers, and present information repeating on a three year rotation. It is probably best to start at the beginning of such books, and work to the end. I have learned quite a bit about both of these subjects because the information changes from year to year; and especially decade to decade. If you wish to accelerate learning in such books, do so by assigning what you feel to be an acceptable level of performance for a child's worst day. For example, if you are blessed with texts which provide a prescribed amount of reading followed by a half a dozen review questions, assign that section with the review questions as one day's assignment. If the child is motivated to do so, he may choose to do the next section as well.

We found ourselves in a jam our first year of home school, because we had borrowed a variety of books from one of the school districts in the area, and the administrators naturally expected that we return them at the end of the school year. Because we had taken the first two months of school to properly present the previous year's information, we found that by May, we still needed to complete more than a month's worth of material. We rewarded our son for the additional time and reading in the following ways:

☺First, we explained to him that the book needed to be returned to the school and that he wouldn't be able to finish it unless we did something about his progress. We additionally stressed that this was no shortcoming of his own, but that it was the result of overlapping 6th and 7th Grade material in September and October.

☺Second, we offered him the option of completing two or three assignments each day. He was still required to do the reading, but by completing two assignments, he would only have to do every second question in the text. By completing three assignments, he could choose three questions to answer in each section, leaving him with the same nine questions he would normally have to answer. With the additional work came additional freedom for him to choose. Predictably, he did not always choose what he perceived to be route to the shortest answers, but those he thought were more interesting or thought provoking.

☺Third, we offered him the option of not completing work in one of his enrichment electives through the duration of the completion of the courses in question. He did not take that option by his own choice.

Spelling books are always started at the beginning and taken to the end. As I mention elsewhere, we complete two worksheet pages a day followed by a day of writing the words five times each. In a cumulative spelling test I give about every three months (usually on days I choose not to teach the rest of the curriculum), I will dictate about 70% of the most difficult words given in each chapter. All three of the children score above 90% for retention. The practice really does make a difference. The usage solidifies the word in their minds for the proper placement of the words in their vocabulary, and the repetition solidifies the spelling.

Reading/literature books remain an enigma with me. I have yet to find a core reading program that I totally appreciate or even particularly like. I guess I have selective memory, but I remember reading as a pleasurable, non-threatening subject. When you, as a parent, are choosing material for your children, remember that the values, goals, and ambitions of your family may be different from those of the contributing authors in Basal Readers. Generally, stories presented in Basal Reading programs are arranged least to most difficult. What has to be remembered is whether the stories are closed-ended character-building plots with socially acceptable outcomes, or whether the writer has attempted to give the child food for thought in a way which might prove eventually to be destructive. If the child is left with a forlorn, lost, empty feeling after reading his daily assignment, the story must be discussed with him or her. Do not allow your child going to bed feeling that the world is an inherently bad place to be, and that there is no hope for the future. Help him or her to express his or her feelings, then discuss possible outcomes. Or, better yet, read ahead in your child's book, choose the stories you feel socially uplifting, and delete from his or her assignments stories which you feel might depress your child or make him fearful.

In reviewing a possible Reader for your child, note the type of illustrations presented for your child. Are they contemporary, full of life, and generally healthy and happy? Do the stories have uplifting and fulfilling chapters? Is this the type of literature you would wish to relax with? Make sure your child is not being manipulated by someone's attempt to take an important stand on an issue that has been wheedled in to a basal reader by a person trying to change society or misinterpret situations to incite anger or protest. That type of reading can come later when a child is emotionally stable enough to make his or her own decisions. Social morality can be taught in the home. Who says a parent can't teach a child not to lie, cheat, steal, be a bigot, racist, murderer or rapist? Literature books need not serve this purpose for your family unless you wish them to. Chapters can be skipped in any or all of your textbooks if you are the teacher.

An obvious alternative to a core reading program is to challenge your child to read classic literature or current literature you have previewed, then dividing the book appropriately. Then you may either question your child orally about his reading for the day in discussion (if you have time), prepare a worksheet for each day's reading, or come up with a form which would best evaluate the progress for each day. This is an option that many home schooling parents have taken. Many parents opt not to review comprehension on a daily basis, but to ask for oral or written book reports as practice after the literature has been read through to the end. This works wonderfully well for an established reader, but can be devastating for a child who is attempting to read or write at a level above where he should be. Remember to be reasonable about your expectations and thoroughly review the literature before your child is exposed to it.

Remember that as a home schooling parent, you have the singular right to step in and put a stop to anything your child is learning that you disagree with. We find that the best platform for our values and views occurs when we encounter literature, science, or social science information that we have disagreement with. We, as parents, can gather our children around us in the evening and discuss what has been read with the entire family and verbally examine, with our children, exactly what it is that we find fault with as well as the pieces we truly agree with. You also have the flexibility to skip that chapter, avoid the issue, and go on.

For Kindergarten, or First Grade, it is you who know your child best. If you really don't know where your child stands developmentally, start at the beginning and work to the end of the curriculum you have chosen. It is important that a K-1 student learn

BOOK REPORT

NAME _____ TODAY'S DATE_____

  NAME OF BOOK_____

  AUTHOR_____

  No. of Pages _____

Name of Main Character_____

Name of Two other Characters_____

Setting of the Story_____

Theme_____

Was there a message or moral? If so, what was it?_____

_____

Synopsis_____

_____

_____

_____

_____

Why did you like the book?_____

_____

What didn't you like about the book?_____

_____

On the back, tell me something about the book that I didn't ask you in any of the other questions..

to hold a pencil, recognize letters and numbers, then do something with this information. Many children pick up the shapes of letters and numbers and have that information in their heads quickly; but are handicapped by their inability to hold a pencil in their hand.

As I have mentioned before, my son's first handwriting looked like he wrote with mittens on his hands. To get an idea of just how frustrating it is to write with hands and fingers that won't cooperate, try to write your signature wearing a pair of ski gloves. Now, imagine copying the alphabet with the same pair of ski gloves on. This is how your young child probably feels. They know they are clumsy. They know their letters don't look like the examples you show them. Hand-eye coordination can be taught, but not in one week, not in two, but after months, or maybe years of practice. Don't expect your little boy to perform like your little girl, or the boy next store; because it just doesn't work that way. If we were all carbon copies, we wouldn't be individuals. Our individual development is just that - different and apart from anyone else's. Don't expect too much - give information to your child every day, and watch for gradual results that both of you can be proud of! Don't rush! Learning will happen before you know it!

Remember - Learning is MAGIC!

-*30* -

ADDITIONAL READING
EXPERIENCES

"There are two kinds of books; those that no one reads and those that no one ought to read."
H. L. Mencken

Get into the habit of reading to your children. As strange as it may seem, even older children can learn about patterns of speech, inflection, expressions of emotion, and proper pronunciation from hearing a parent read a good book. I find that it is a good chance to catch up on the classics I didn't have the time or the resources to read as a child. My parents were not readers, and consequently did not keep many books in the house. As a child, I read avidly, and checked as many books as possible out of the school library, but I realize that we have been provided with so many works of wonderful literature that one person cannot possibly read everything that has been written.

We have gotten into the habit of frequenting local bookstores. It is equally as fun to visit the library regularly. I generally choose a book at random before I enter the section I set out for in the first place. I am seldom disappointed. Once you are accustomed to reading, it is easy to realize that you can read for your own pleasure and it takes nothing away from you or your family. Set aside time for yourself which doesn't interfere with anything else you are doing. My husband and I read in the evening while we are waiting for the kids to go to sleep. It gives the children a certain sense of security knowing that we are awake while they are going to sleep, and that we will check out funny noises that would normally worry them. It also affords us an opportunity to unwind. The proper literature at the proper time should induce relaxation and a sense of well-being. If that is not the case, you've probably chosen the wrong book. If you are more upset with the world after a half hour of literature, find another book. We have found that our vocabularies have increased greatly, and that we wake up fresher after we have spent time reading in the evening. We find that taking our minds off business for an hour or so before sleeping helps us to sleep better.

Books are treasures that can be shared. It is fun to read passages from a new book to the children the next day. This often encourages them to take up the same appropriate literature; after you've finished the book, of course! In short, it is best that your children see you reading and know that you read for pleasure. Its simply a good example, as long as your choices are a positive role model.

Know what your children are reading. In general, it takes from a few minutes to a few hours to review literature under a third grade comprehension level. It is truly best to know who is influencing your children. Take the time to review the information in the Author's section. If this individual is someone you would not care to meet, or, worse yet, might have a negative influence on your children, you might consider passing up the title before you spend the money or waste your child's time.

There are two Newberry Award Winners with which I have great disagreement in general principle. One of my daughter's former favorite authors included in one of her novels an explanation in detail of how a pre-teen stole a credit card from a parent, used it to order plane tickets, picked up her boarding pass, and ran away from home. Even my daughter expressed concern that the consequences of the protagonist's actions were dangerous, stupid, and bordering on criminal. Why would any adult wish to explain such a repeatable and easily accessible crime--in detail--to children?

In another of her books, this award winning author carefully detailed how a child unwrapped birthday gifts to peek inside before the celebration, then lie to cover her actions. Nobody has to explain to anybody that these things can be done, but why on earth would a children's author write such a thing? Read your childrens' books. Some of them are very interesting, uplifting, and filled with beautiful, artistic illustrations which are worthwhile as art. Some are not.

Have your children read classics. In general, these interpretations of life have been read so many times by so many educators, parents, and children, that they are relatively safe for children. They are also a representation that life is very circuitous.

Lucy Maude Montgomery; though now deceased for nearly three-quarters of a century, knew intimately most of the people I know. Character types have not changed, and social customs, while skewed from time to time, generally succumb to the same pressures in thirty or forty year cycles. My daughter recognizes her aunts, uncles, cousins and friends in Montgomery's characters. While the same may not be said for Dickens, most of us can point out the same wrongs in society which charged his novels with emotion. While we may not actually believe that Toad could walk, talk, and cause trouble, we can recognize that *The Wind in the Willows* (and its new, and most wonderful sequels, *The Willows in Winter* and *Toad Triumphant* by William Horwood) are a representation of the most valuable friendships of all---those brave enough to help a friend in adversity, and even abject stupidity.

During a parent-teacher conference, I mentioned to one of my children's teachers that we were collecting old copies of classic literature. The teacher gave me a quizzical look and asked me what I was talking about. After a moment, I realized that the poor young *teacher* really didn't know what 'classic literature' was. It is with this in mind, that I have taken some time and listed some of our family's favorite classic literature as a part of the Appendix. Hopefully this will help you to build a reading list appropriate for your family. Remember that much contemporary literature is being written as you read this, and there is always room for additions as time progresses. Do not close your mind to the work of new, young authors.

There is a lot of trash out there, but a few treasures are still being written. Beware of purchasing too much formula fiction for your children, as it can absorb your child to a point where they are reluctant to read the work of other authors. There is so much work out there that reading the same formula stories again and again is a terrible mistake! Likewise, look for trusted authors who are able to create new and wonderful work every time they put pen to paper (or printer), and refuse to succumb to formula tactics.

Another source of an appropriate listing of literature, as I have mentioned elsewhere, is from the local school district. Most school boards have put together grade level literature lists for students in their district. Books listed here may contain information you may feel inappropriate, but most literature approved by the schools will be found in school libraries, and should be relatively close to your expectations. The key here, is, again---if in doubt, read it before your children do.

More promising, still, would be a list of required reading from a respected private school. Many colleges and universities are now requiring a list of reading from students upon entrance, and because private schools are quite competitive, they update their lists frequently. In addition, private schools usually do not recommend literature unless a staff member and parent committee-member has reviewed the work for appropriate content, social value and morality, unless the work is considered a classic timeless in value. This resource listing would save a bit of work for the discerning parent.

Be aware that even works that are considered classic literature may contain language or situations you may not believe appropriate for your child's age. Because so many home schooled students read above grade level, you may find that your child is ready for adult level vocabulary, yet adult situations and language may be quite inappropriate or inadvisable. Again, check the work for content before accepting someone else's opinion. Learning to trust your judgment can save you the embarrassment of explaining age-inappropriate concepts to an academically precocious youngster.

-81-

TEACHING MUSIC

"After silence that which comes nearest to expressing the inexpressible is music."
Aldous Huxley

Anybody with a musical instrument, record player, tape player, television with PBS, or CD player can teach music, as long as the opportunity of the proper outlet for a well-rounded education in music is provided. By well-rounded, I mean you are cheating if you present only music that you are personally in touch with and feel good about. Your children hear your favorite music frequently. Admit it. My children listen to classical music because I like it, and so does my husband. That's what we listen to, and we spend a lot of time teaching it, in addition to other things.

There are all sorts of music available to play, sing or listen to, and one of the best ways to discover different types is to provide your children with varied opportunities to listen or participate in uplifting music, including opera, classical, contemporary jazz, blues, country-western.....you know the list.

We were in the fortunate position of being in the right place at the right time when one of the local school districts decided to cut their school budget by completely *eliminating the music programs* in all of their schools. I was shocked, but first in line to buy the books when the district had their jumble sale. Unfortunately, many school districts are opting out of their music programs, and they are getting rid of their music texts. Don't let them go to the dump. They contain information. And whether you use all that information or not, most of it is worthwhile, and can be an enriching part of your child's education.

There are some options, though, if you don't feel up to teaching music. Consider music lessons of some sort for your child or children. I have never visited a town or city without at least one qualified music instructor, or someone, like myself, who has played the piano for years, and can at least teach your child to read music or explain musical notation. This is worthwhile, because, piano lessons also teach math theory, and through my piano work, I developed an unusual speed on the typewriter and computer keyboard. Since I am not a concert pianist and make no money with my music, my skill should be useful for something! There are many acceptable alternatives to pianos such as keyboards, rhythm instruments, flutes, clarinets, recorders, violin, voice lessons....you name it. Or you could teach your child to play the harp....which is a great deal of fun, and relatively easy (believe it or not!). Its also picturesque.

We listen primarily to non-lyric classical music. Listening to Classical and Contemporary Classical music, it is said, contributes to a mind's ability to think on several different planes simultaneously because of its complexity. We often enjoy a variety of this type of music by many composers and encourage our children to learn about the composers lives and to learn to play their music on piano, flute, clarinet, Indian flute, dulcimer, and/or harp, depending on the nature and source of the work.

Being conversant in the language of music is a special gift you can give your child. Being conversant regarding the origins, theory, composers, and history of music is an important asset and should be a key course of study for all students, especially those who are college bound. Liberal arts requires the study of the arts. The sciences require an understanding of applied science, therefore music, in this context, would be the study of mathematics, wave motion, and physics as it relates to sound.

-32 -

THE DARK SIDE OF
MUSIC, ART AND LITERATURE

"You know that the beginning is the most important part of any work, especially in the case of a young and tender thing; for that is the time at which the character is being formed and the desired impression is more readily taken...Shall we just carelessly allow children to hear any casual tales which may be devised by casual persons, and to receive into their minds ideas for the most part the very opposite of those which we should wish them to have when they are grown up?

We cannot...anything received into the mind at that age is likely to become indelible and unalterable; and therefore it is most important that the tales which the young first hear should be models of virtuous thoughts...

Then will our youth dwell in a land of health, amid fair sights and sounds, and receive the good in everything; and beauty, the effluence of fair works, shall flow into the eye and ear, like a health-giving breeze from a purer region, and insensibly draw the soul from the earliest years into likeness and sympathy with the beauty of reason.

There can be no nobler training than that.".
Plato's Republic.

If you are a parent who feels that it is okay to ask your child to close the door when the stereo is on in his or her room, or if your child walks around with a walkman plugged into his or her head, thinking that your child is entitled to listen to whatever kind of music he or she wants to, it might be wiser for you to pay close attention instead of ignoring the problem. This is not the 60's and the government does not censor lyrics for our children anymore. **Popular Music is different now than it was 10, 15, or 20 years ago.** And you should know about the difference. I didn't know how different and how deadly until recently.

If you disagree with me on this, please, for heaven's sake, and for your child's sake, read or listen to the lyrics of the songs your children listen to. Don't shut out their music, because your kids and the people they buy from may tell you something you don't want to hear and that you should be hearing. These people may be telling your child something that may be potentially deadly, even if you don't suspect it. It could destroy their lives. Quite literally.

I have, so far, mentioned the changes that occurred in our lives when we started to Home School, and some of the incentives we had to home school, but the saddest and most horrible of all involved the son of a dear friend and business associate. Because this was a turning point in my life and my husband's life, we knew that we had to change something in our lives, or we could conceivably lose one of our children.

When the teenage son of our friend was found dead of suicide on the floor of his apartment, music was playing on his CD player. The CD that was in his player at the time of his death was played at the wake we attended. The result was heartbreaking. While I know the name of the group he was listening to, I do not and never will know the name of the album, and hope I never hear it again, because many of the songs contained vivid *instructions and descriptions* of ritualized suicide. All of the other songs on this album actually glorified maiming, rape, and grotesque forms of death.

This young, brilliant, college student, who had been a former Eagle Scout, talented artist, and Honor Student had been lured to his death by popular music. I came to the chilling realization that many of my friends do not realize that their children are listening to the same dangerous garbage packaged as music, literature and drama. Under other circumstances this young man had a bright future, but he will never realize his potential.

It was this incident, combined with the drug-related death of another young son of a second business associate which solidified my conviction that we, as parents, must spend as much time as we possibly can with our children, and that we **must know what our children are doing, and who is influencing them,** and do not leave that up to chance. If nothing else, I feel that this was a personal message to me that there is **an acceptable alternative to peer pressure and negative socialization.** For me, and for my family, **the answer to my fears, questions and concerns was in Home Schooling.** And for many reasons since I made this life-changing decision, I am glad every day that I made it. Whatever sacrifice I make daily for my children (and I do not believe that this is a sacrifice at all) does not compare to the kind of sacrifice these children and their desperately bereaved families made during 1994.

To those two families who lost their children during 1994 due to peer pressure and outside influences, we thank you for the knowledge that your children gave us, and understand very deeply your hurt and loss. We thank you for making our decision so clear to us. Your children may have saved our childrens' lives. It is, further, my hope that this message can reach out to other, yet unsuspicious, and yet heartfully caring parents.

I hope you will take the time to listen to your children, and their music, and that you will sit down and read what they are reading. Join them as they watch what they are watching. Know your kids, and know their friends and their friends' parents. Know the danger signs which should alert an awake parent to severe problems such as depression, violence and emerging anti-social behaviors. Even if you don't make the decision to home school, please know what your children are doing when your back is turned. It could save their lives and save you the agony of losing someone you love dearly at some point in the future.

Unfortunately, many non-home-schoolers have interpreted this concern as a wish to shelter our children or keep them from knowing about sex, drugs, gangs, tobacco, alcohol and other negative influences. Quite the contrary. It is important for us, as it is for all of the parents we have met, to introduce these concepts in a controlled, calm, informative atmosphere...before they encounter the drug deal-ers and other bad influences. Rather than by exposing our children to these negative influences, we wish to inform our children before exposure to dangerous situations so that they can properly protect themselves when the time comes. It is not, then, a matter of *Just Say*

No, but knowing when it is appropriate to say *no*, and when to avoid a situation which would require an emphatic *No*.

A friend once observed that she didn't have the luxury of being with her children all the time, so she would just have to trust them to do the right thing when the time came, then deal with the problems as they come up. This about a three year old in day care and a ten year old in the public school system.

Hiding our children in a safe vacuum would be a horrible mistake, and this is recognized by most intelligent home schooling parents. Being able to spend enough time with our children to talk with them openly, honestly, and with appropriate questions and informed answers is a luxury we purchase with the time we spend in educating them academically and tolerating the comments from people who don't understand our situations.

The difference we can make for our children is in giving them the time it takes to ask the questions, then researching the answers to provide them with the information they need. We can also *not* explain anti-social or dangerous behavior in terms of *choices* as has become popular in public school settings, but rather in terms of modern, intellect-based *taboos*. Providing living, real examples of people who have destroyed their lives with drugs, those who have died terrible deaths of cancer or venereal disease, or telling our children the eventualities involved in alcohol, drug, and sex-related personal abuse can be the examples which will eventually save their lives and save us, as parents, the horrible grief of burying a child.

-88 -

COST

> *"Law of Inflation: Whatever goes up will go up some more."*
Kin Hubbard

Prepared curriculums are relatively expensive when compared to the cost of textbooks purchased used, but quite inexpensive when compared to the cost of a private school teaching the same curriculum. New textbooks are expensive, and teacher's editions are extremely expensive when purchased one-off as you must do when home schooling.

My philosophy on cost is that I have a clear conscience about spending money on my children. Unfortunately, we are not a family of limitless wealth. We have checked into the already-over-crowded private schools in the area. We don't like what happened in the public school, and while we are budget conscious, we know what we would be paying for a education given in a private school. Where else could we get a 1/1.5 teacher/student ratio?

There is always an answer to any difficult question. Ours came in discovering a wholesale book warehouse and the used curriculum sales at the schools. Learning from pre-owned textbooks doesn't bother us or the kids, and I'm glad of that. My feeling is that a book is only a resource of knowledge. It is only useful if it is read. It is a shame to throw away a book that has gone unread.

You can expect to pay: (Remember, these are all estimates, but will give you an idea of what you may pay for the following)
$ $25.00 to $50.00 per book for a **Student Textbook purchased from a School Textbook Manufacturer**

$ $135.00 to $200.00 per book for a **Teacher's Edition of a Student Textbook** (Keep in mind that up until about fourth or fifth grade editions you may not need the TE's unless you are unsure of enrichment materials, or need additional help in planning your curriculum.)

$ $75.00 to $400.00 per student per subject for **Student Textbooks and Teacher's Editions** from a prepared curriculum manufacturer. Remember, again that while you may not feel that you need the TE, that the curriculum manufacturers will probably include the Enrichment materials and course materials lists in their TE cost and try to discourage you from splitting up their sets. You may want the enrichment materials, but make sure this is your decision.

$ $7.00 to $15.00 per **Consumable Student Texts** which may include K-2 curriculum textbooks (usually consumable workbooks) for Math and English, and K-8 Spelling. This may also include workbooks which may be issued to accompany Reading, Science, Social Studies, Math, Foreign Language or English Books. They can be an important resource for mid-chapter review and practice and are usually well-worth the investment. Reproducibles can be copied so that if you sell the textbook to another home schooler, that family may also use the materials. Make sure that you check the nature of the copyright before photocopying any material.

$ $5.00 Seems to be the going price for **Wholesale** pre-owned Student textbooks obtained from a Wholesale Warehouse. Of course, this pricing may vary with the person you deal with in your area.

$ $35.00 Seems to be the going price for **Wholesale** pre-owned Student textbooks with TE's from a Wholesale Warehouse in our area. At this price they are a steal and well worth it. Be prepared to prove you are a home schooling parent if attempting to purchase TE's from an outlet where the staff doesn't recognize you.

$ **Consumable Student Texts** that are bought at a **Wholesale** outlet can vary, but, as a rule, will be generally less than the $7.00 to $15.00 for new ones. You may have to leaf through several editions before you find one that is not marked up, but it may be worth the extra effort. I have found them for free or for as little as $.50. Sometimes they are more expensive, so be sure to ask if in doubt.

$ **School Districts** will charge whatever they can get for **Student Texts and Consumables**. There is very little predicting this. The last sale I was at charged $.25 to $1.00 per textbook and about

$.10 per consumable. In some cases, I noticed that the ladies in charge took pity on us for buying over-used and falling apart textbooks and didn't charge us for one or two, but in general, it is never a really great idea to continually ask for discounts, especially when you are dealing with people who intrinsically want to do nice things but have to follow rules. It is never a good idea to try to make people feel sorry for you because you are an overburdened homeschooler. A play for sympathy will not work...and it shouldn't. Some districts will charge more, and others less. The reason they charge you will be either to satisfy the taxpayers that they are receiving something for the books they originally paid for; or they are paying the people who are sitting there collecting the money. Otherwise, they would charge nothing and take them to the landfill, which nobody really wants to see happen!

$ The best and cheapest place to find textbooks is from **other home schoolers**. In this arena, everyone seems to know the rules, and generally, while most home educators will want to recoup their investment, you probably won't walk away feeling cheated. As a bonus, you will get advice about the curriculum from someone who has used it, understands it, and can explain its complexities or idiosyncrasies.

We have found that books, and in particular, textbooks, are never a waste of money, but that we should never waste money on them if we can find a bargain on something we know to be reliable. Don't rush in your purchases. Buying to save time is always a mistake. Take the time to make an intelligent purchase, and you will have curriculum to last through each of your children, or even, perhaps, for your grandchildren.

-*34* -

GRADES

"The world is divided into people who do things-and people who get the credit. "

Dwight Morrow

I have already discussed my philosophy regarding grades in reviewing the Assignment Sheets and Cumulative Grade Reports, but as a matter of personal philosophy, I'm not big on grading my kids. My two older children always wanted to see where they scored, and, as I've mentioned before, it is probably a good idea to write some information down about what we are doing. I have also discovered that the University enrollment officials here in our state are gearing up to require some sort of documentation of progression when they enroll home school students. Be prepared to do some paperwork. If you have some standardized forms to use, this becomes second nature.

I use a strict percentage scale the same as my teachers used when I was a kid. Let me reiterate:

90 -100% ➜ A
80 - 89% ➜ B
70 - 79% ➜ C
60 - 69% ➜ D
59% ↘   ➜ F

No matter what the grade, my kids are still required to correct anything they have gotten wrong, and in general, they are expected to do it completely, and on their own. I will give them a general explanation, but I don't play games with the kids, and I don't do their work for them. Our emphasis is strictly on learning. Our kids aren't rewarded for their grades, and never have been. Their reward is their knowledge, and they are very proud of themselves for successfully completing textbooks and learning the material. So whether they get a 95% or a 70% on a daily assignment, they are required to take another look, and master the skill before they move on. Sometimes the key ingredient in the chapter is the 5% they missed; and the 70% may have resulted from the misunderstanding of one key definition. They know this is important, because they don't want to attempt the next assignment without understanding yesterday's. To do so always causes more headaches than skipping the corrections solves. They grasped this concept rather quickly.

We do not have nine-week grading periods, we do not have semesters, and, unfortunately, we don't have end of year parties. But what we do have is interested learners. We have lunch as a family in a restaurant each time a textbook is completed. If it is a major textbook and represents a leap into a new school year, we dress up and go somewhere nice for dinner. We don't buy them expensive sports shoes, clothes, or (heaven forbid) toys unless we have a reason other than schooling to give such items.

The kids determine their own extra credit, and they are praised in comments from my husband and myself. Particularly good work is always praised. We try very hard not to be judgmental or hard on them when they are having a particularly bad day. We expect the corrections the next day, but there is no punishment. I wouldn't want to be punished for not understanding something, and neither would my children.

As a little reward to the kids, I keep a box of self-adhesive reward stickers next to me while I'm grading. It also helps me tell at a glance when all the corrections are made in a consumable book or notebook, and I think the kids enjoy looking through and seeing what weird stickers I've found. Its become a challenge to find goofy, inexpensive stickers to use in grading. I have found the most useful are the holographic stickers that shimmer as I leaf through their notebooks. Its easier to find my place each day.

In addition, as I grade, I use sticky notes to mark pages that need grading, both in the textbook and in their notebook or workbook. This leaves a good trail for the kids to follow, and makes it easier for me to figure out where their work is to be re-graded.

-*35* -

SEPARATING PARENTING FROM TEACHING

"Reform the education system by giving all parents the right to choose their children's school and insist on a value-based education where virtues such as integrity, responsibility, industry, morality and courage are taught.

It is time we put our children first. Our families and our nation depend on it."...

Dan Quayle

In operating a business in partnership with my husband for the past eleven years, I have been asked invariably, and by almost everyone, "How do you separate your business life from your family life?"

Since I started homeschooling, I have been asked invariably, and by almost everyone, "How do you separate your teaching time from your parenting time?"

The answer to both questions is the same. I don't. Maybe other people need to, or believe they need to separate segments of their time into categories, but I find that too confusing. That is why we accept business calls at 10:00 in the morning on Sundays. It just doesn't matter. It is all a part of our life. If my kids ask me a question, I would be compelled to answer it the same way whether I were teaching them at home or sending them to school. It keeps me from becoming schizophrenic.

I personally believe that it is a parent's right and duty to shape their children with positive images and to provide proper guidance. That seems to be the same goal that teachers should strive for. What parent *isn't* a teacher?

In order to become a teacher for a previously public or private schooled child, the job is harder than just deciding to be a teacher to them. First, a parent must earn a trust that most teachers naturally have, unless, of course, the child has learned to mistrust teachers. If the child has learned to mistrust everyone, the problem becomes almost insurmountable but not irretrievable.

For example, what if everyone lied to you about everything? Well, of course, that doesn't happen. But look at it this way. What if these things were said to you regularly, *every day*, with the following resultant actions from a *child's* perspective:

✔"I'll be with you in just a minute, honey, as soon as I finish changing the baby" (Mom forgets to read the *Winnie the Pooh* story and goes to the bathroom, then finishes fixing dinner) Mom lies...or is she just busy?

✔"I'll be right in to tuck you in" (Dad goes into the kitchen, gets a drink of water, returns to the bathroom to brush his teeth and into the family room to watch television - nobody tucks Shari in.) Dad lies...or did he just lose interest and forget?

✔"Sit down and be quiet for a moment while I finish grading the papers, then I'll help you with the math problem" (Stuck on Problem #6, Sam doesn't finish his assignment because he honestly believed his teacher was going to get back to him. He turns in the uncompleted assignment the next day, gets an F and an admonishment from the teacher who promised her help, then forgot). Teacher lies... or was she distracted?

✔"I'll bring you your coke in just a minute, big guy" (the waiter, seeing that his customer is only a kid goes on to take an order at the next table and forgets to bring the beverage). Waiter lies...or did he have a demanding grown up to take care of?

✔"Yes, Mother, Sam really liked the blue coat with the purple polka dots that you gave him for his birthday" (Sam is overhearing a phone conversation about something he told mom he *hated*). Mom lies...or was she trying to save someone's feelings?

This is not willfully vindictive behavior. These adults merely forgot, or were saying what they thought was expected of them under the circumstances. Its not a sin --- *or is it?* You see, adults are very accustomed to taking advantage of children that way. But what the children see is that their needs, their wants, and their thoughts and wishes usually get cast aside when an adult is dealing with them. In similar situations, as adults, such behavior, taught at a young age by example, can result in divorce, lawsuit, or jail time. Perjury is a crime, as is non-compliance with a written contract. Teaching children to put others off, even by example, is a dangerous precedent to set .

Unfortunately, we are all guilty of doing this to a greater or lesser extreme. Its part of being a parent - part of being an adult. But when it is repeated over and over day after day to one extent or another, children are taught by the age of eight that grown-ups usually lie to them. *And, believe it or not, this is how children learn to lie.* This is also how children learn to mistrust adults. They watch us and they trust us to do the right thing, then at some point they realize that things don't always work the way they're suppose to...even if the child has lived up to his part of the bargain. And that is where we get into trouble.

I cannot say that I have never forgotten to respond to one of my children's requests. I also cannot say that I have never lied to save someone's feelings. But I can honestly say that when confronted with my mistake, I have responded in the most honest, forthright way possible, at least, eventually. And if I know that I have been perceived as having committed an unfairness to my children (whether or not I personally feel that I have---and this is important) I apologize. My children apologize, too. They have learned that from their parents.

We have, in this way and in all other ways, established that while we, as parents are fallible, that we are willing to recognize our mistakes and are willing to work through them. It also shows a willingness to recognize other people, to express empathy for their situation, and to provide an outlet through which we can grow, change and learn. It is disheartening to notice how many people in contemporary society are unwilling to say the two words *"I'm Sorry"*.

My son's sixth grade teacher told us proudly, after having shortchanged our son in a very important way, that she *never changes grades* (okay, I can understand that reasoning) *and she never apologizes. For anything.* (Oops! What happened to being a positive role model?) How many of these people influence our children each day? Well, its hard to say, but they are more insidious and dangerous than we might think, because, as I said, as adults, we are *always* teaching the children we encounter. You see, by definition; physically, emotionally, and mentally, they are looking to us for guidance, and they deserve honesty and fairness.

For my own edification and for off days when I need something positive to look at, I keep a three ring notebook with page protectors around for quotations of all sorts. I write down quotes from all sorts of places. I have a favorite quote by Roald Dahl, *(Charlie and the Great Glass Elevator)* and another from A.A. Milne *(Winnie the Pooh - See Chapter 36)*, and the collection grows almost weekly, even though I'm not sure the kids are aware it is around. One of these days, I may add this to my list of things to make the kids do on my days off. Maybe I can make them memorize one of my favorite sayings so that they can repeat it to me. Or, maybe they can make collections of their own. Most of the quotes in my collection are funny, some of them serious. Most are short and to the point (which is something I will never be)! Most of these quotes, though, carry some sort of reminder of fallibility and a sense of responsibility for action, thought, and social presence. Sometimes even *Winnie the Pooh* can help put problems into perspective.

-*36*-

ESTABLISHING TRUST

"A little consideration, a little Thought for Others, makes all the difference."
A. A. Milne

Our children are not born bonded to us. This theory is shot down every time we read in the paper about a baby dropped from a seventh story window, or a young mother who drowns her beautiful child out of social frustration. Unfortunately, there is no law that says we have to love the children we give birth to. We have to *learn* that. They, too, have to *learn* to love us. Trust must be established. It must be reestablished and reinforced when home schooling starts, especially for a previously schooled child, and most exceptionally for a child who has attended day care. Unless you have discovered a mystical place where all of the day care workers are over paid, love their work, and get to know each and every child intimately and are expressive and joyful each and every minute in their love for their charges, daycare is a hard place to grow up.

As I mentioned above, it is important never to lie to a child. It is important to express love and devotion to a child, and it is very important never to hurt a child, either emotionally or physically. To do so destroys the trust. If a mistake is made, it is important to follow it up with a definitive apology. Your child will learn from this. Your child will also learn if he is hurt in any way and there is never an apology. This hardens a child to other people's needs and pain. Often neglected and abused children become abusers themselves. I consider this a sobering thought.

My *first* attempt at home schooling was an absolute

disaster. Faced with placing my not-yet-ready-for-school five year old first child in Kindergarten for the first time, we opted for a private school. We were disappointed to find that his teacher was having severe marital difficulty and was taking her frustration out on her male students - most particularly our child, because he looked much like her own son. We discovered, also, that this was because he lacked proper motor coordination to provide her with the completed written assignments that she required, and that, we determined after several years of soul-searching, he wasn't ready for. After catching chickenpox and missing two weeks of school, we were contacted by the school and informed that he had flunked kindergarten.

"How can a child flunk kindergarten?" we asked.

"Simple," the administrator told us frankly, "he has missed in excess of 10 days."

The next question should have been

Do all children who catch chicken pox flunk in this school?

I was too timid to ask that question, but I was not too timid to pull our son out of that school in March. I began to home school him, according to the parameters dictated by that private school.

It was our goal to assure that he could read by the time he started first grade, that he could perform four digit addition and subtraction with carries, and that he could write within the parameters of a second grade pre-lined notebook page. Anyone with any experience knows that these are demands not easily met by a child with fine motor coordination problems and only five months to fulfill them, but that was the recommendation, so I tried. For four months. Then I met the vice-principal of the local public school who told me that I was trying too hard, and that she would match me up with a first grade teacher who really could teach our son most (but not all) of these things, but that even she would take at least nine months to do it all.

You see, I failed miserably at my first attempt because there was so much for both of us to learn, the greatest of all was patience, and the ability to accept that children need to be taught bits of information in each subject every day, and that there are limits to attention spans, little fingers, growing minds, and mommy's temper. When he didn't learn, I would start to yell, catch myself, then leave the room. Thank goodness that as a young mother I was told to lock myself in a bathroom rather than hurt my child, verbally or physically, as a result of frustration. I'm afraid I wasn't a very nice person the first time around and I hated myself every minute for doing things I knew might be wrong for my son. But I meant well, and, hopefully, didn't do too much damage psychologically. At least Sean's first grade teacher was able to undo what I had inadvertently done wrong in my ignorance, and was able to teach him happily and well. This angel is now a school administrator. Her influence and insight has helped literally hundreds of children and their parents over the years.

We must promise ourselves that in order to establish trust with our children, we must never ever do any harm. No yelling, kicking, screaming, hitting, or name calling. We learned these rules in kindergarten, and they are still true for us as parents!

-87-

ABSENTEEISM

"Achilles absent was Achilles still.".
Homer

When I was ten years old and in fifth grade, my family took a family vacation from our small town in Illinois, through Arizona, and on to Anaheim California to visit Disneyland. I came home with Whooping Cough. (Yes, I had been vaccinated. The vaccine failed.) Not only was I absent from school for the two weeks on vacation; but I was also absent for additional two months while I was dreadfully sick and recovering from a really nasty and potentially fatal disease. In this time, though, I received straight A's. These grades were not gratuitous, although I received a wonderful and unexpected gift.

The gift I received from Mrs. Lawrence, my fifth grade teacher, was the ability and the knowledge to home school my own children almost thirty years later. Each day my sister picked up my homework which was intricately organized and agonizingly complete. I had assignments in each subject, both reading and writing. My teacher scrupulously corrected my spelling, grammar, and handwriting in addition to the core requirements. This was something she did **not** do for her thirty-odd other students. It was the year in which I learned to recite the fifty states and their capitals in alphabetical order. I can still do it, and it is probably one of the few things I will ever memorize. I discovered sentence diagramming, learned all about Beethoven and how to chart square dances from the music teacher, and learned the chemical composition of most rocks and minerals indigenous to the Midwestern United States. She kept me busy and she kept me happy. She made me feel special by writing special, reassuring messages to me and by sending messages from my friends. Most importantly, she taught me that children can be self-taught with the guidance of a caring teacher, even if they are lonely and would otherwise be bored, frightened, or feel helpless with their circumstances.

One problem we were having while my eldest son was in public schools was the frequency of his illnesses. Unfortunately, he seems to have inherited my tendency to pick up anything that is going around in the shopping malls, at the grocery stores, and in the schools. We have had a few bouts of colds, flu, and three pneumonias through out years of home school, but we have lost very little time, because if the kids choose to work (and they choose it, because it is something interesting for them to do instead of being bored), they can work in bed, and they have an understanding mother to tell them when to rest, or to give permission to continue working 'just a little longer'. It is wonderful to be able to be there for them and to know if something goes wrong and to be glad when things go right.

Most parents will encourage their sick children to do something with their time during days off from school. I encourage my children to do as much as they can, and knock off when they start feeling so lousy that they can't. We don't have absences. We don't have to provide excuses to anyone, because we make the rules and enforce them. We can do this as long as our children are learning. I will never flunk a child and make him repeat an entire year because he has been sick.

Absenteeism due to a vacation is not a problem with home school because there are so many interesting places to go and so many interesting places to learn. A trip to Hawaii can mean time with an astronomer at Mauna Kea, or walking across the crater of Kiluea-Iki after calculating the mid-point of the flight from Los Angeles to Kailua-Kona. Even a trip to Disney World™ can mean time spent at Epcot Center™ exploring scientific advancements, the dinosaurs or the World Showcase, or taking the short trip to Cape Canaveral.

Exploring the world with the kids on vacation can be the most enriching experience a parent can have, as it opens our eyes to the world for another 'first time' adventure -- through the eyes of our children who see things so very differently than we do!

A vacationing child is not absent from learning!

Susanne L. Bain

-88-

FIELD TRIPS

"I am the ruler of all that I see."
Yertle the Turtle

Since my husband is an Architect, he spends a great deal of time in the field on job sites. We have the freedom to take the kids, and depending upon the stage of construction either explore what is being done, or find an alternate place to be during my husband's meetings. It has worked out quite well.

One advantage of home schooling is that while we are out with the kids, many other children are at school. We can go to malls, zoos, libraries, art museums, national parks and a variety of other places. We find ourselves, for the most part, alone, except for solicitous adults willing to explain things to our kids once they understand that they are home schooled and genuinely interested.

We find that our children are rather more willing to ask questions than when they were publicly schooled. There is no one in our group who will ridicule them for asking a stupid question, because we recognize that there is no such thing as a stupid question. We answer questions every day and recognize the right of our children to expand their minds. They have learned to say things like *'excuse me'* and *'pardon me'* and *'thank you'* once the questions have been answered, and we find that other adults respond in a positive manner to this approach. Our children were never taught to say these polite things at school. They were, however taught the phrase *'Shut up'* from teachers and other students. We don't use this phrase in our school. We think the phrase *'Shut up'* is counterproductive.

This is not to say that our children run rampant over forestry service employees, unwary art curators and talented Navajo weavers who are concentrating on their intricate patterns. They seem to have developed the same innate ability to sense when someone is willing and ready to respond to them---just like any other polite, socially aware adult. They also know when to watch quietly.

We have had a number of wonderful experiences with our children over the years, and they may serve as examples of Field Trip experiences you may wish to enjoy with your home school students.

✿ We have visited **Ancient Native American Ruins** in Northern Arizona, explored the homes where they lived and raised families, visited the streams where these ancient people fished, rinsed their food and washed their clothes. We have seen where they built their fires, and the kivas where they appealed to their deities. We have walked through the museums and seen weavings and pottery over a thousand years old and experienced their art through the eyes of our children and with expert professional explanation from a forestry service representative who did all this with our family just simply because we explained we were home schoolers. She treated our family as she would have an entire classroom of thirty or sixty kids. Just because we asked.

✿ We have visited **Libraries**, bought used books, checked others out, watched our children talk to librarians, use the computers, and find out things for themselves with very little, if any, supervision. Our kids understand why they need to be quiet, because they understand that they themselves do their best work when the house is quiet. If they see others working they express empathy through their actions.

✿ We have visited **Construction Sites** and watched as footings were dug out of pure granite, foundations pinned to cliffs, slabs poured, framing and drywalling complete, and owners moved in. All in a period of eighteen months to three years, and with projects they watched their father develop, draw, and supervise.

✿ We have visited **Zoos**, where the children talked to experts on snakes, raptors and geologists who treated them with respect and answered questions...because we weren't there on a busy weekend with lots of other otherwise uninterested adults and anxious and undisciplined children crowding us out.

✿ We have visited **Disney World®**, where our children spent a week exploring **Epcot Center®** and **Discovery Island®** because *they* preferred to do that instead of spending the majority of their time on thrill rides and in arcades.

171

✿   We also had opportunities, through our home school group, of visiting **a candy factory, a potato chip factory,** seeing the workings of a **supermarket**, and attending several **Little Theater** presentations.

✿   We were treated to a backstage tour of an **historic theater**. Our children were trusted to sit at the sound desk with the electrical engineer, climb the catwalks, manipulate lighting and special effects.

✿   My children, as home schoolers, were offered opportunities to undertake trips to Australia and New Zealand, attend camp in Colorado, and to participate in local choirs, home school orchestra, and children's and adult theater presentations. As you can see, we are not bereft of opportunities for exploration and enrichment.

Exemplifying good behavior can get your children into places where you never would dream of taking a child. We have been invited to all sorts of places to tour, to learn and to have things explained to us that most other people don't know. And we get invited back because our children know how to act. People remember us, and they remember other home schooled children. In a small, expensive china shop in the best of all locations in Scottsdale, we were asked to *please visit again soon*. On the west coast of the Island of Hawaii, in a shop that sold primarily glassware and one-of-a-kind original art, we were asked when we would return. These gallery owners correspond with me regularly.

Think of the places you visited on Field Trips as a child. As a child, I imagined what it would be like to return there alone, or with my family. In most cases, we never went back. Imagine every wonderful place you've ever visited on vacation. Each of these adventures has the potential for education and enrichment for your child. You have to be willing to allow yourself to be your child's teacher and to explore and become excited without the self-consciousness we often feel as we explore the concept of being an *authority*. Buy the guide books, look at the maps, and do something unusual. Go to a volcano instead of a beach for a day...look through a telescope at the top of a mountain instead of buying souvenirs. You and your children can choose the adventure for yourselves. Once you stop being embarrassed about your excitement, this becomes easy.

-*89* -

TEACHING YOUR CHILD TO THINK

"Wisdom is not wisdom when it is derived from books alone."
Horace

I've already reviewed how to teach your child to learn, but one of the best resources on the subject of teaching anyone to think is a book they probably won't want to read at first. Take the time to read one of two books by the same author, Edward deBono: *New Think*, and *Lateral Thinking*. It has become required reading as an adjunct to upper level advanced math programs in many of the better private schools, and by many of the brighter math instructors in more progressive and successful public schools. I believe that the idea of 'lateral thinking' is a valuable aid in helping a child to develop not only creatively, but also to develop his or her mind, and prepare it for adulthood. The second of the two books is (I believe) still in print and, as a paperback, is a relatively inexpensive addition to a personal library. I highly recommend it.

All of us, as adults, are capable of having opinions. It is now, from what I understand, socially incorrect to pass this information on to our children. But if we are not allowed to pass on our opinions to our children, is it also possible that we are forcing them to *reinvent the wheel* every time they encounter situations which, as I said earlier, repeat about every thirty to forty years? If we were not aware of the holocaust during World War II, could this horrid thing possibly be repeated? Yes, and it has - in countries where education is reserved for an elite few.

173

If we were quiet about the results of dropping Atomic Bombs on human beings, is it possible that some third world nation might experiment on its own, or our, population? Yes, and it has happened. **Spread the word! We all must know and pass it on!**

But, knowing about the bomb and knowing about massacres and ethnic cleansing really isn't enough, is it?

There are many times when everything in our house (including our business) comes to a screeching halt when one or both of us recognize that it is time for a *talk*. We sit quietly and comfortably in our living room and discuss our opinions on subjects from politics, professional courtesy, respect for adults, arthritis, to the proper care, feeding and treatment of small animals. Usually these lectures are triggered by some problem we are having. Sometimes, they are spurred on by the behavior of our friends or business associates. Sometimes, we explain our own actions. And sometimes we disagree so wholeheartedly with something written in a textbook that the anger pours out in the form of our explanation of the proper way to provide information in an acceptable manner.

It is okay to do this. We have built our family around this. We can, as I have mentioned several times already, mold our children's minds to attempt to do the right thing. Sometimes merely giving it a half-hearted try and failing just isn't enough if the action has a far-reaching ramification for someone or something. Not feeding the dogs is not acceptable, because the dogs will starve, and they count on us to take care of them. Screaming in department stores and throwing temper tantrums is not acceptable behavior. Watching someone starve to death and not helping him to learn to feed himself is wrong, but so are some ways of handling starvation, when that starvation is forced and is a form of social manipulation. Even our youngest son joins these conversations to offer insight and opinion.

If we reprimand, we feel an obligation to explain our reasoning. Our reprimands are not followed by **BECAUSE I SAID SO**, which was the explanation I always got, followed by another swat. We don't hit our kids. We will not hit our kids. We never have hit our kids. We feel an obligation to the world not to do so, because we firmly believe that to hit is to teach to hit. Remember, we are teachers. We are doing something our parents were told they could not do. We are raising polite, well-trained, drug, alcohol, and tobacco-free children in today's society without violence. That is not to say that we do not lose our tempers or sometimes raise our voices. After we calm down we explain.

'Because I said so' is not an adequate answer for an action that we commit that we would never allow our children to commit. Just because I'm bigger than someone else doesn't mean I can take advantage of him. But it does mean I have a responsibility to give a plausible reason for my actions. I know that one is now, and eventually all three of my children will be bigger than I am, and I hope that I have trained them not to take advantage of me as all of them become larger physically.

Shaping a child's mind and helping him to reason things through involves an opportunity to watch someone else reason through similar situations. When we encounter something that our children have never encountered, we explain it to them. Including our mistakes. Hopefully some of what we have learned and can explain will rub off.

☞To drop a picture frame means breaking the frame, and sending glass shards all over the place. If that happens, it is not safe to walk around in bare feet. I will, in addition, have to spend money on a new picture frame. The lesson? Please don't play with my new picture frame because it may break, and someone will have to clean up the glass and buy a new one.

☞Don't write in ink on my sofa. We had to spend money on our sofa, and it is difficult to remove ink from the upholstery. We like our sofa and would like to keep it. Please don't use the pen anywhere near our family's sofa again, or I will become upset again.

Sometimes short, and to the point, and sometimes launching into an hour's dissertation, we are striving every day to spread as much of our experience around to our children as possible. We can only hope that the majority of it sticks, and that our children will be able to survive in a changing world when they have need to and to transfer knowledge from one situation (our mistake) to their future challenge (their triumph).

-40-

CONCEPTUAL LEARNING

"To the small part of ignorance that we arrange and classify we give the name knowledge."
Ambrose Bierce

I cannot memorize anything. I can, however remember having been able to in certain circumstances. I know I learned the names of the states in alphabetical order, and memorized complicated musical compositions. It was not easy for me. But I always did really well on theme papers and essay tests, because while I cannot easily remember bits and pieces and details of information, I can remember the general idea. I remember that President Lincoln and U.S. Grant were presidents of the United States and that both of them were adults during the Civil War. What I don't know is the dates of their births, deaths, or presidencies. But I know where I can find that information if I need it. You can easily identify a conceptual learner in your home. These are the people who

✔cannot memorize a song on the piano, even though it is practiced hundreds of times, but can hum the tune or sing the song, or can play the tune in the 'wrong' key.

✔cannot memorize the names of States or capitals, but knows where to find the information very quickly.

✔and can relate people and places with other people and places, but not to dates and specific times.

✔may be able to recognize that they know someone's face, but can't put a name to it, even though this person may be a celebrity or a relative not seen recently.

It may indicate that, rather than being learning disabled, they may just learn differently than some other people do. It may also indicate that complicated learning is going on and this information takes less precedence than other facts. Unless your child wishes to be a historian or a particularly glib life of the party, remembering things as groups of information may not be as big of a handicap as many other shortcomings could be. While I advocate exposing children to details, such as dates and lists of information, it may not be totally necessary to force them to remember the information verbatim. In some cases it is mandatory, and may force you to think rather laterally of a solution to the problem. It may be possible that you may succeed only in putting history in order for your child. Teaching key words, drawing time lines, studying maps and globes, and enabling them to find information quickly as they need it may be a more promising goal for you. In addition, finding an alternative method of teaching may successfully portray the information in a form your child will understand more easily.

Remember that grasping concepts has many practical applications, and teaching the value of key words, and the availability of reference material and how to use them is as important in teaching as Reading, Math, or any other core subject. The use of Reference Material is an art which can be manipulated through books, periodicals, library research, and the internet, and will later be a prerequisite for college success. Practice in all of these practical applications is invaluable and to be encouraged no matter which type of learner your child may be or where they are bound professionally!

-41-

ALTERNATIVE METHODS OF HOME SCHOOLING

"Experience is what you get when you didn't get what you wanted."
Italian Proverb

As I mentioned early on, it is important to remember what I have outlined here is a rough journal of methods we have developed, experimented with, and borrowed from others over our years of home schooling, and of some of the experiences that have brought us here. But there are many methods of schooling that are equally as effective, and may be more efficacious for you, your family, and, most importantly, for your children. Any of the options I have mentioned previously could be perfect for your situation, and I have come in contact with so many warm, loving home teachers and their children that it would be quite difficult, if not impossible to include them all here.

The common thread among most of the home schoolers I have met over the years is a desire for independence, safety and increased stability and learning for themselves and for their children. I have met

♥A mother who told me in no uncertain terms that she couldn't fathom why anyone would wish to purchase a 'canned curriculum' when nature presented such wonderful food for thought and the library was so rich in literature and reference.

♥A gifted mother of seven's *unschooled* sixteen year old who entered college last year and carried a 4.0.

♥ A mother who told me that her son spent an entire year studying both sides of the Civil War, and wrote his Whole Language styled curriculum himself. He designed and sewed uniforms for both

Union and Confederate soldiers, that he was able to wear during a play he wrote and for which he had constructed all the sets, produced scripting and cast all of the secondary roles to friends and acquaintances.

♥A mother, who distributes a line of home schooling books who uses nothing but the Enrichment books that she sells to support her family, and whose children were bright, ambitious, knowledgeable and happy participants in learning and in their home business.

♥A mother whose ambition was to re-shape the structure of the school system her children attended while protesting by home schooling her children until her vision of an Arizona Charter School came true. Her children were both re-enrolled in the school she championed - one at grade level, and another a year ahead. She has since again left Arizona and is home schooling in a different state because her husband was transferred to a new position. I suspect she will fight her battle with a new state legislature.

♥A mother who disagreed with the policy of her daughter's school to the extent that she removed the child two months short of eighth grade graduation. She successfully finished the school year with her daughter and met the stringent requirements of an exclusive private school for fall entry.

It is easy to see that the common thread among home schoolers is a true affection for their children. When asked why all sorts of curriculums and styles are so successful, my response is uncommon love and dedication of the parents who earn the trust and perseverence of their children. These are all options, dissimilar to mine, with different goals, and very similar outcomes. Most of these students will either go to college, a university, or enter their chosen professional field through experience or apprenticeship. If we, as home schoolers can all strive for the same united goal - and that is to create happy, well-rounded, socially adept, moral, ethical, learned people, who can support themselves and their families in later life, I know that we will leave our society in good hands. Don't you think?

-42 -

THINGS TO REMEMBER THAT SCHOOLS USUALLY TAKE CARE OF FOR YOU

"I believe that what a woman resents is not so much giving herself in pieces as giving herself purposelessly."
Anne Morrow Lindbergh

There are a variety of things that become more complicated when a parent decides to home school. Included in this list are some records and responsibilities that we don't necessarily think about in our every day life if we aren't reminded to do them by someone else. But as adults who are taking on full responsibility not only for our children's lives, but also for their education, we will be expected to make sure that these requirements (among others) are met:

✔**Immunizations** must still be made, and **Immunization Records** must be kept. As with an infant or toddler, there will be no one around to remind you that every four years or so your children will need certain booster shots to assure that they don't catch diseases that, unfortunately, still run rampant in our world. Whether or not your children are going to school, it is important to remember that we can still take our children on vacation, to malls and restaurants, and, in places where there are people, there is always the risk of illness. At some point in the future, too, if your child wishes to enter college, the military, or many other professions, they must have *proof* that their shots were kept up to date as children. The responsibility for this record keeping now falls solely to you as a parent.

✔Remember to take your child for **medical check-ups** at reasonable intervals, if not annually. There are many things that could conceivably go wrong with a child, that we may take for granted, and which should be checked out. Generally, doctors know better what to look for than we do. As home schoolers, too, it is easy to become complacent because our children do not contract as many diseases as other children because their exposure is generally limited to other healthy children and adults.

✔Keep track of your child's **Birth Certificate**. Whether or not your child is in school, it is important to remember where you put it, so that it can be conjured up if and when you need it, whether to copy and send with the Affidavit of Intent to Home School (or other similar form), to enter college, or to expedite a marriage license.

✔Think about starting a **College Fund** for your child. $10.00 per week adds up to $520 per year plus interest if you can afford it. This might eventually be enough to provide for the early college education your child may earn because of your efforts, or help you provide textbooks if there are no other funds available. You might consider investing wisely in a conservative investment portfolio so that your investment can grow along with the child.

✔Remember to make sure that your child sees a **Dentist** at least once a year to assure his or her dental health. It is hard to learn with a mouth that hurts all the time. Some children don't even know that their little mouths aren't suppose to hurt and won't complain.

✔Have your children's eyes checked professionally by an **Optometrist or Ophthalmologist** roughly once a year, especially after growth spurts. The reason I mention this here is because our son's near sightedness was first noticed by a music teacher, and not by us. This is the sort of thing that is easy for a parent to miss.

✔Think about and teach your children about proper nutrition and consider teaching a course in **Health Education** each year.

✔Be prepared to talk to your child about **Sex** and related issues. Again, this is a prime opportunity to make sure that your child understands your point of view and not the perspective of peers who may have misinformation or dangerous ideas. What works well is a discussion that takes place in the comfort, safety and privacy of your home where questions and concerns can be talked out with enough time for everyone and a genuine attitude of caring.

-48-

PUSHING A CHILD TOO HARD

"It is always one's virtues and not one's vices that precipitate one into disaster."
Rebecca West

I know that one reason why other people resent home schoolers is that we always tend to talk about home schooling as though it were a cure for every evil imaginable in society. It is not that, but it is another alternative answer to some problems inherent in the way our society is structured. It is only one alternative; but it can be played out in many and varied ways.

I have already described my misadventures with my oldest child in my first attempt to home school, but I am and was not alone in my folly. It is easy to recognize parents who enter home schooling with the plan of pushing a child beyond grade level into a situation that they may later regret.

In former chapters, I have cautioned that it is not a very good idea to tackle too many lessons a day, nor is it a good idea to skip information in search of other, more advanced, information. It is also not a particularly good reason to approach home schooling with the intention of teaching Algebra, for example to an eight year old who has not yet mastered basic addition, subtraction, multiplication, division, fractional equivalents, decimals, and graphing techniques (among other things). All of these skills, by necessity, come together in upper level mathematics.

I know that at this moment in time, I could teach any of my children the theory behind many advanced disciplines in a few weeks or months. I refuse to do that because I know that in order to fully comprehend mathematics and utilize it properly and professionally in later life, there must be a depth of knowledge not attainable unless the child is truly comfortable with the information that feeds the equations and calculations. This goes for many other subjects as well. To force feed any information to a child is inherently incorrect, but to gradually work through what must be known first to what can be known after that is understood is a more logical and common sense approach to anything. I must learn to dig a hole, moisten it, fertilize, and mulch it before I can put a plant in the ground. If I miss any of these steps, the plant will not be successful. It is much the same with knowledge.

Knowledge without a basis is a knowledge that is not deeply understood, or, for that matter, useful. While I realize that textbook authors are fallible and human, I also know that these people have spent a great deal of their lives digging up information for their work. Much of that information will build a core of understanding that will blossom when connected with other information later in life. Hopefully this core of varied knowledge will eventually become knowledge on which to build a professional lifetime.

It would be wonderful to think that our own children could develop talents more quickly than other children, but human development is relatively predictable, and can only be manipulated to a certain extent. We need not rush our children into adulthood to satisfy our egos, or the egos of our children's grandparents. Take your time. There is a lot of wisdom out there for the kids to absorb, and we all learn a little bit at a time. Our children will be on their own in the world soon enough and we have a lot of work to do.

It is common for an exceptional student to burn out in the public schools, and more prevalent in competitive private schools and at a college level. In the past few years, I've seen this burn out in home schooled children more often than I have originally thought possible. Establishing trust and reasonable expectations is a much more feasible goal than striving for early entrance to college or for Algebra mastery at the age of eight.

-44-

LEAVING THE WORK FORCE TO HOME SCHOOL

"To nourish children and raise them against odds is in any time, any place, more valuable than to fix bolts in cars or design nuclear weapons."
Marilyn French

I have many female friends whom I respect who must, for one reason or another, work to either support, or help support their families. They lead difficult and complicated lives, just as we, as home schoolers lead very difficult and complicated lives. Each family, and each individual must carefully weigh important decisions which will affect their families and those around them.

I must say that I am in an enviable position of being able to make a decision because the work that I perform as a gainfully employed, bill paying, taxpayer can be performed at home in bits and pieces, and I have a very understanding and supportive husband to work with.

There are many women (and men) who are home schooling who are doing so without the full support of their spouses. Making a decision such as pulling children out of school should not and can not be taken lightly or made independently. The manner in which your children are educated should be of primary importance to both parents, and therefore should be discussed thoroughly.

As I have mentioned earlier in the book, we originally decided to home school for many and varied reasons, and we know, deep inside, that we are doing the right thing for our children for this moment and for our circumstances. Each day, we see examples of all of the reasons we home school and are grateful for our opportunity.

Rearranging your life as well as your *lifestyle* may be possible for you, but the sacrifices must be reasonable sacrifices, and the reasoning behind the sacrifices and the lifestyle changes must be apparent and acceptable to both you and to your spouse. I must say that without the support of my loving husband that it would be next to impossible to juggle the responsibilities of home schooling my children, and I have listened to many stories told to me by home schooling mothers who develop problems because their husbands feel that 'they don't do anything with their time.' Frustration, many times translates into an unfair comments from spouses who

✔Do not understand how much actual time is spent teaching children.

✔Cannot cope with sudden total financial responsibility.

✔Does not understand that it is a full time job to merely run a household that is full of people twenty-four hours a day.

A clear and concise dialog must happen between family members (including children) at the onset, or during discussions of the decisions surrounding home schooling issues, because, many times, it means the possibility of leaving behind a portion of, or the total sum of financial support of one spouse. This can lead to family disharmony which could conceivably outweigh any benefits to be gained by home schooling, or any other reason one may choose to leave the work force.

In order to put things into perspective, there are many things that cost money that may be bypassed in switching from a professional/office/outside work situation to home schooling which do not make themselves apparent until many months later.

✔Pressure to *look professional* changes. Although I wake up in the morning, do my hair, and wear appropriate clothing, these clothes are much different, and cheaper, than those clothes I needed for   the specifications service I ran before my husband and I consolidated our businesses, or when I administrated other people's offices and had to show up for work in an office each day.

✔Children do not have to succumb to *peer pressure* and preferences for over-inflated designer labels. Children can dress comfortably and without self-consciousness. As I've mentioned, my kids wear what they want to and are comfortable. They're not embarrassed to wear shorts and a plain t-shirt if that is appropriate.

✔Pressure to purchase new vehicles becomes secondary, in many cases. I know of women who literally work to support a family's weakness to drive new and expensive automobiles each year. In the average two car family, most people purchase or lease one new car each year, believing payments are rightfully a fixed expense. This is not necessarily so. There is a tremendous and constant marketing pressure to change vehicles frequently. We have circumvented this by paying off the vehicles we have and driving them until we know that it is probably not safe to do so. With the advent of bumper-to-bumper extended warrantees, this probably increases the life of a car to approximately eight years. This is not popular right now, but we feel it is the bit we can do to help save the earth, and it has definitely been a boon to our financial condition. It is nice not to have car payments. In addition, mileage on our vehicles is not an issue because we're not driving the kids to school every day, though we have other obligations.

✔There may have to be a sacrifice in the way of 'extras' that an extra paycheck can bring the family. These things include, as I've mentioned, expensive clothes, shoes, and cars. But also, they include things like frivolous trips to malls (which you may find that you don't have as much time to do, anyway), large allowances for your children (if you don't drop them off at the mall, and they don't eat lunch at school, where will they spend the money they have?), and eating in restaurants frequently. I guess I quantify this in my mind as "needs" and "desires". Once you start categorizing your purchases in this way, the fuzziness starts to clear and it is relatively easy to see which things can easily be sacrificed and which can't.

When considering leaving the workforce, you may wish to consider some of the following suggestions:

$Pay off your car. (I know---this is a very difficult one!) Obviously this may suggest that a trade be made for a smaller or less expensive model, or maybe a slightly used vehicle you can buy for cash or a smaller monthly loan. Beware of re-financing to lower your payment, because you will undoubtedly end up with a longer time in which to pay off your new loan with increased interest debt. This would defeat your purpose. Also beware of trading down into large repair bills.

$Pay off all of your **short term debt.** Credit cards and Department Store Cards - Anything with a credit limit. This may involve a promise to yourself and an agreement with your spouse that neither of you will use your credit cards until they are paid off, then pay them off each and every month. If you don't cheat, you have your credit under control. Several years ago, we cut up most of our credit cards. That removed temptation to use them. Whenever possible, write checks or pay cash. Avoid using the credit for any purchases except emergencies when you don't have the cash.

$Watch your children's spending. Help them to decide what is important and what is not. This may be the hardest part, because we all want to do what is proper for our children. A pair of $35.00 shoes probably provides the same serviceability as a pair for $150.00. It just doesn't have a designer logo on it. Explain to your children that the goal here is to cover their feet and protect them; not to provide additional unearned income and advertising for merchandisers and manufacturers .

$Make a list of fixed expenses that keep your house going that you may be able to decrease somewhat, but will in no way be able to avoid even after everything is paid off. **Budget** things such as:

Rent/Mortgage	Electricity/Gas
Water/Sewer Fees	Telephone
Trash Collection Fees	Taxes

Know how much your family spends on each of these items. Unfortunately, the only way you can affect what you spend on fixed items will be by making a conscious decision to live in a house where everyone agrees to **turn off lights** and **save water** when they are not needed. **Turning the thermostat up or down** to save electricity or gas may be a sacrifice everyone can live with. According to our power company, changing the thermostat by as little as two degrees can save a certain amount of money. **Fixing leaks** and **limiting shower time** may save you water, and running the dishwasher and washing machine only when full also helps. But remember, there is a limit to how much you can save by limiting utility and "fixed expense" items.

But there are other ways to save money, if you are determined. Remember, you still have to have somewhere to live, some way to communicate with the world, feed your family, and be able to wash your hands and face regularly. Since there will be someone in the house 24 hours a day when you are home schooling, you may not realize the type of savings you are hoping for since someone else has been paying the utility bills at your office and at school if you and your family have typically been away from home nine hours each day.

$Food is another 'designer' item that we had to control on a budget. We don't purchase pre-packaged or pre-prepared food, nor do we eat junk food. This started in our family relatively recently; but we are thrilled that we did it. Fresh vegetables, fruits, and meats are generally cheaper to buy and prepare. We seldom turn on our oven. We grill, saute, and eat crunchy, fresh things. Being home with your children will keep you from having to purchase pre-packaged snacks and beverages for lunches. This has saved our family a tremendous amount of money over the past few months, and we have found that we have lost weight (my husband more than me, unfortunately) and our children are more alert. In addition, seeing you and helping you to prepare healthy, fresh meals will influence your children to grow up healthier, and perhaps divert future weight problems. Having your children help you prepare food and the family table, you will be doing their future spouses a favor, in helping them to learn to become independent, self-confident adults who don't run to fast food restaurants for every meal.

These are only ideas. When my husband and I feel that finances are affecting the way we feel about ourselves and our family, we reassess our goals, and take into account what we are doing and why. The goal of working (at least in our minds, and you may not agree) is to provide shelter and food for our family. That is really the only reason to make money, other than saving for retirement. If not for having children, my husband and I could probably live just about anywhere and live off the land (although we are not survivalists).

As foreign and strange as it may sound, the goal of working outside the home in someone else's office or place of business is not necessarily the achievement of success, personal advancement (especially in someone else's business, because you are there to make money for someone else), or to buy a new car every year. A resounding comment made to me once by a mother who took a job at nights to supplement her husband's income goes through my mind every year at Halloween. "Having my new job is allowing me to buy the $60 butterfly costume Stacy wants this year for Halloween." Since then, she has held a forty hour a week job, spends little time with her beautiful daughters and is grossly unhappy and doesn't know why. Last year, not having spoken in several months, we received a letter with her Christmas card proudly announcing that her oldest daughter had finally come out of drug rehab. But she and her husband are always showing us their new cars. Every year.

If you can honestly reevaluate your expenses, take an honest look at what you can do without discomfort with your anticipated change in lifestyle, it may be possible for you to leave the workforce.

As a home schooling parent, you will not be wasting your time. You will not have to think of yourself as a bored housewife, because there will be no time for boredom. Though it is socially unacceptable in many areas of the United States to be a stay at home mom, I think, as well as a growing number of men and women in this country believe, that we, as parents must grasp any opportunity to spend time with our children. This will keep them off the street, slow down the rate of growth in gang related violence, and hopefully keep some kids off drugs. You can, in addition, provide an education for your children which can truly transcend that which is offered in public, and, unbelievably, some expensive private schools by merely being around, answering questions, and providing on the spot guidance for your closely held children. Secure children who perceive their learning environment to be safe will grow up to be secure adults who can function in a world that is, admittedly not so safe. Home schooled children tend to be independent, happy, and productive children who can then grow up to be ambitious, productive adults. It is from these types of individuals that creativity and advancement flows.

-45-

WHAT ABOUT COLLEGE?

"Knowledge without sense is double folly."
Baltasar Gracian

Each time we discuss home schooling with our friends and other people who care about our family the question of college and university study comes up. This was certainly a concern of ours, and we consequently spent much phone time and wrote many letters to college and university presidents and discovered that, to many, the SAT test scores represented more to them than a high school diploma. What we were told, by the local community college president, the university president's office, and our favorite private college president, is that home schooled children in their colleges seem brighter, pay better attention, and do generally, higher levels of work because they have been taught how to learn and are thought of as self-motivated.

We have developed our teaching methods with the help of these individuals and with the advice of others who either hold advanced degrees, are successful business people in control of enormous mega-corporations, or both. We have also taken advice from young mothers and fathers without high school diplomas who are successful business people in their own right, as well as everyone in between.

We have been invited by two community colleges and two private colleges to enroll our children when they are ready. When asked about the absence of a high school transcript or diploma, they reiterated that their requirements were more in line with the satisfactory completion and scoring of standardized testing and suggested ability to learn. This is what standardized testing indicate. In addition, for home schooled students, these colleges required personal interviews with admissions officials and essays which exemplified the level of comprehension and writing ability of the student.

We learned from several of these conversations that there is very little respect among those in charge of higher education for the wide-spread gratuitous grading policies of many public high school teachers. In addition, we were encouraged to keep a cumulative grade record, keep written record of the textbooks our children have completed, and have our children attend personal interviews with the school administration when the time came for enrollment.

We were told that when our oldest son was ready for upper level mathematics he would probably be ready for enrollment. This time came sooner than I was prepared, but at a point where I approached the threshold of my abilities with him. We enrolled our oldest in an out-of-state college within a few days of his sixteenth birthday and watched him grow as a young man.

Although it would indeed be a feather in my cap to have my youngest son enrolled in college at or before eleven (and according to the school, he could be, at least in Mathematics), we will probably delay his entry because of his size, his maturity and the inconvenience of ferrying him back and forth twice a week for a 1-1/2 hour class. When our children are ready for college, college is ready for them. I am thrilled to have their professional expertise to fall back on. The criteria that they require, at present, is the testing requisite to any college freshman in the diagnostics for placement. He will have to take the same tests as everyone else, just like his older brother and sister.

The Arizona Federation of Home Educators, which sponsored our yearly convention this year holds a summer group graduation for eighth and twelfth graders during their convention or at a local reception hall. For our family, providing, for our children, an opportunity to wear cap and gown and be honored in such a way is worthwhile. In addition, AFHE sponsors prom each year in conjunction with graduation. I think it is a nice touch and might be something to look for, organize, or request of your local home schooling group.

My best advice is to find the college or university of your choice which offers the courses and degree programs your child's future will demand. Discuss, with Admissions the possibility of eventually enrolling a child you plan to home school. Let these people know that you are concerned and genuinely plan on providing learning situations. You may even wish to discuss the type of curriculum plan you have decided to use. Don't talk to a secretary or assistant. Make sure you go to admissions professionals or counselors or you will come away from the phone call with the unfulfilling notion that you may have received the wrong information, or information you cannot trust. Having a secretary tell you that home schooling is all right and hanging up isn't nearly as nice as having a college president or dean of students take the time to actually discuss the institution's requirements with you. In the meantime,

✔Keep Cumulative Grade and Attendance Records.

✔Keep Written Records of Textbooks Completed & Grades.

✔Approach the college which provides the degree program your child prefers - don't settle for less or for an alternate program.

✔Talk to an administrator, admissions official or counselor knowledgeable about the degree program your student has chosen.

✔Prepare your child and have him take PSAT, SAT, and/or ACT tests as required by the schools you are considering. Have your child aim for a score of 1200 or greater on his SAT.

✔Fill out an admissions application.

✔Have your student write an essay, whether required or not.

✔Check financial aid availability. Put your finances in order if your child will attend a private college.

✔Put student's medical and immunization records in order.

✔Find your child's birth certificate.

✔Request and attend a personal interview with admissions officials. Let your student do the talking.

✔Make sure your child has competent skills in grammar and composition, math, and general knowledge. Check requirements for pre-admission and meet those requirements - again, keep records.

✔**Do not argue** about your child's competence with anyone connected with the college of your choice. Be firm about facts, but accepting of their advice. If admissions suggests a year at community college before reconsideration, simply ask why they recommend that course. That is not necessarily a rejection, just a suggestion - and it may be a good one.

Good Luck to you and your student!

-46-

Until The Pendulum Swings.....

"The only thing that makes life possible is permanent, intolerable uncertainty: not knowing what comes next."
Ursula K. LeGuin

I honestly believe that things will get better with our public school systems. In the years since the first publication of this book, and the almost eight since I began home schooling my children the success of the home school movement has caught the attention of the news media, the teacher's unions and even the legislature. In addition to my home school efforts I have attempted to stretch my personal influence by becoming as politically active as my limited discretionary time would allow. Two million families already home school and the 15% of the population considering home school can't be all wrong.

Unfortunately, most of the home schooling parents I have met seem too meek to attack the moral dilemma anywhere outside of their own homes. I can understand this, because the first line of attack on immorality, ignorance and ethical decay should be in the home. As a matter of fact, it worries me to watch as friends, family and acquaintances stretch themselves in the name of volunteerism and to the detriment of their own children and marriages, yet ignore what is happening in their own homes to their own children.

As long as teachers fail to understand and take seriously their position in the community as role models and learning facilitators, we will continue to have schools bankrupt both academically and morally. Lack of discipline, low test scores, and lack of knowledge will continue to be the nation's major problems, as from these seeds stem criminality, ethical decay, social disorientation, and poverty.

193

As long as national security was threatened through the World Wars, Korea, Vietnam and the Cold War our government took a stand, recognizing that through our children we could attempt to solve the problems created through national emergency. This generated a true understanding and search for truly gifted children to accelerate academically and provide interested minds to send on to our Universities and later produce the technology and philosophical leadership needed by our country in times of trouble. There was no time for political correctness in an unsure world, as there was no room for gratuitous grading, and the wrong time for gratuitous award of scholarships to low-achievers with a sports background. Fine minds were accepted and molded into greatness through a strong educational environment which strove for, rather than ridiculed intellectual prowess, excellence and genius. Our government as well as the thinking population of our country recognized that without the fine tuning of these young minds that our democracy would not only suffer; there was a realization that Democracy could and might fail. And nobody in their right mind would want that to happen.

It was through the recognition that we, as a nation, could quite conceivably become another republic under the governorship of the Third Reich, Japan, Communist China, or the Soviet Union that our academic machine strove to assure that our children understood the need for strong minds, strong bodies, and strong morality. It is sad to realize that it is only under the flag of dire threat that our country would rally in favor of the education and proper upbringing of our children to stand behind the efforts of strong families and schools.

Commercial television, popular music, academic structure and even some of our formerly respected religious leaders are now encouraging an attitude of non-competition, mundane performance and immoral, unprincipled behavior. Most importantly many of the respected medias are actually encouraging ignorance, corruption, and lack of ethics. This unfortunately sometimes comes under the headings of non-judgmentalism, political correctness and tolerance.

Until the pendulum swings back to conscientious behavior and intellectual incentive within the average family in the United States, the pendulum cannot swing throughout the world, because we set the standard and the stage for most of the negative and the positive that happens throughout the world, with the possible exception of Asia, which is now the most academically powerful region of the planet.

Asian nations now perceive western civilization both as a threat as well as a growing economy to be manipulated, and many of our political analysts and indicators are finding that their gain is, in many cases, our loss. The average Asian parent knows what the average American parent does not - our children are falling behind, and theirs are stepping ahead-with the help of *American* technology and through the imitation of cold war era American education! With that knowledge, they are carefully creating knowledge ownership for their children, and their children are excelling, using the same teaching methods our government insisted on during the fifties and sixties.

It is an undeniable fact that the family continues to be the nucleus of all that happens. Both by coincidence and plan, I have had the pleasure of meeting, speaking with, and listening to United States Congressional Representatives, U. S. Senators, local politicians, our world famous sheriff, several mayors, two state school superintendents, as well as the CEO's of several major corporations and many of those people in charge of the print and broadcast media. I have spent many hours talking with and listening to teachers and school administrators. The common denominator that all of these interested and vital people have described as the biggest problem facing the United States and the world is the deterioration of the family, lack of respect for marriage, and the common move for adults to ignore, belittle and abandon our children.

As an individual interested in Home Schooling, you are, by definition, an unusual and open-minded person who can make a difference by involving yourself in some way to improve the future. If only by spending the time with your own children to make them moral, decent, thinking individuals in a two parent loving family you have already done more than 70% of the population of our country is willing to do. This cannot be half-hearted or part time, though it takes very little effort. Though the gains are not monetary and cannot be measured by the type of car parked in the driveway, the effects are long-lasting and incredibly satisfying. The average person does not lie in her death bed wishing she had worked more during her life, but, rather, wishing she had spent more time with the important things...the people she loved - her children.

This is not only accomplished by Home Schooling. If you opt, for any reason, not to home school your child (and there are many compelling reasons not to), you can still make a difference by taking a genuine and concerted interest in what it happening to your child at school as well as at home, and at the same time seeing to the responsibilities that make your family work.

As I have mentioned, I have witnessed over-volunteering as an excuse for child abandonment, frustration, guilt, child abuse and marriage destruction. The first volunteer organization you should join must be your own family. We can limit the number of charity situations by providing strong, supportive families to absorb much of the workload of these agencies. Remember the primary nucleus of our country is the unbroken family. The center of the nucleus is the strong marriage that keeps the unbroken family whole. A new car, new shoes, or a larger home will not accomplish this, unless that larger home is in a better neighborhood where influences are more positive. That option does not always work either, as many of the same problems occur in every neighborhood and in every city.

I have seen that by merely talking with people who help to mold and make decisions about education and government locally and nationally that impressions can be left which can actually facilitate change---or at the least, create an interest.

Although I doubt that my children will be able to reenter the public school system, I remain hopeful that things will change - that the percentage of marriages failing will decrease dramatically - that fewer children will be neglected and left to founder during hours when their parents simply don't care about them, or perhaps don't have the time to properly attend to them - and that teachers will be taught to teach and to think positively about their students, and that they will do so without complaining bitterly and constantly - that school administrators will spend time on campus doing the work they are paid to perform during school hours - and that curriculum will reflect an ongoing stress on academic excellence. Someday all these things will come to pass. I hope that there will be no need for a war - cold or otherwise - to facilitate a renewed light in our educational system. At this point parents can be parents, teachers can be teachers, and our children can grow up and model a society so spectacular that the history books cannot ignore them.

****

APPENDICES
Classics Literature List

Around the World in Eighty Days - Jules Verne
The Call of the Wild - Jack London
Little Women - Louisa May Alcott
Oliver Twist - Charles Dickens
The Adventures of Tom Sawyer - Mark Twain (Samuel Clemens)
Treasure Island - Robert Louis Stevenson
The Wizard of Oz - L. Frank Baum
A Journey to the Center of the Earth - Jules Verne
The Strange Case of Dr. Jekyll and Mr. Hyde - Robert Louis Stevenson
Heidi - Johanna Spyri
The Merry Adventures of Robinson Crusoe - Daniel Defoe
20,000 Leagues Under the Sea - Jules Verne
The Mutiny on Board HMS Bounty - William Bligh
Kidnapped - Robert Louis Stevenson
Great Expectations - Charles Dickens
The Prince and the Pauper - Mark Twain (Samuel Clemens)
David Copperfield - Charles Dickens
The Last of the Mohicans - James Fenimore Cooper
A Tale of Two Cities - Charles Dickens
The Red Badge of Courage - Stephen Crane
The Count of Monte Cristo - Alexander Dumas
Frankenstein - Mary Shelley
King Arthur and the Knights of the Round Table - Howard Pyle
The Time Machine - H. G. Wells
The War of the Worlds - H. G. Wells

Ivanhoe - Sir Walter Scott
The Hunchback of Notre Dame - Victor Hugo
The Jungle Book - Rudyard Kipling
Just So Stories - Rudyard Kipling
The Wind in the Willows - Kenneth Grahame
The Willows in Winter - William Horwood
Toad Triumphant - William Horwood
Hans Brinker - Mary Mapes Dodge
Anne of Green Gables Lucy Maude Montgomery
Pat of Silver Bush - Lucy Maude Montgomery
Little House on the Prairie - Laura Ingalls Wilder
1984 - George Orwell
Animal Farm - George Orwell
Time Out for Happiness - Frank B. Gilbreth, Jr.
Castle Dreams - John DeChancie
The Christmas Day Kitten - James Herriott
Thomas A. Edison, Young Inventor - Sue Guthridge
The Adventures of Don Quixote - Miguel de Cervantes
R-T. Margaret, and the Rats of Nimh - Jane Leslie Conly
All Creatures Great and Small - James Herriott
The Lion, The Witch, and the Wardrobe - C. S. Lewis
The Crimson Fairy Book - Andrew Lang
The Hobbit - J. R. R. Tolkien

Alice's Adventures in Wonderland - Lewis Carroll

Mary Poppins - P. L. Travers

Island of the Blue Dolphin - Scott O'Dell

Yertle the Turtle and Other Stories - Theodor Geisel (Dr. Seuss)

The Tale of Two Bad Mice - Beatrix Potter

James and the Giant Peach - Roald Dahl

The Mighty Human Cell - Patricia M. Kelly

Peter Pan - J. M. Barrie

*Check with your local library to determine when they will be liquidating soiled or mistreated books...this is sometimes a source of charitable revenue for them, and can be a wonderful source of bookshelf books for your family. Also, never throw a book away --- give it away!

READING FOR PARENTS AND YOUNG ADULTS

New Think - Edward deBono

Lateral Thinking - Edward deBono

Demonic Mnemonics - Murray Suid

Body Talk - Myles Callum

The Book of Virtues - William Bennett

Cosmos - Carl Sagan

What Your 1st Grader Needs to Know (through 6th Grade) - E. D. Hirsch Jr.

How to Save the Children - Amy Hatkoff and Karen Kelly Klopp

Peoplemaking - Virginia Satir

The Way Things Work - David Macaulay

The Man Who Listens to Horses - Monty Roberts

Mister Rogers Talks with Parents - Fred Rogers

Imprimis - Hillsdale College, Hillsdale, Michigan

Reviving Ophelia - Mary Pipher

Managing Martians - Donna Shirley

The Schools We Need - E. D. Hirsch

The Children's Machine - Seymour Papert

Standing Firm - Dan Quayle

Pooh's Little Instruction Book - A. A. Milne/Ernest H. Shepard

To Renew America - Newt Gingrich

A Life on the Road - Charles Kuralt

Ender's Game - Orson Scott Card

...So Help Me God - Daniel E. White

8 Real SAT's - The College Entrance Examination Board

The Ultimate Visual Dictionary - Dorling Kindersley

The Gift of Fear - Gavin De Becker

Our Times - The Illustrated History of the 20th Century - Turner Publishing

The Great Gatsby - F. Scott Fitzgerald

The Metamorphosis - Franz Kafka

Death of a Salesman - Arthur Miller

To Kill a Mockingbird - Harper Lee

Farenheit 451 - Ray Bradbury

Brave New World - Aldous Huxley

Gone With the Wind - Margaret Mitchell

Jane Eyre - Charlotte Bronte

The Scarlet Letter - Nathaniel Hawthorne

The Grapes of Wrath - John Steinbeck

Hamlet - William Shakespeare

The Hound of the Baskervilles - Arthur Conan Doyle

Back to the Moon - Homer Hickam, Jr.

Master and Commander - Patrick O'Brian

Trikes - Hal McSwain and Lucien Bartosik

RESOURCES:
CURRICULUM/SUPPLIES

Saxon Publishers - *Texts*
2450 John Saxon Blvd.
Norman, Oklahoma 73071
1-800-284-7019

Christian Liberty Press - *Texts*
505 West Euclid Avenue
Arlington Heights, IL 60004
www.homeschools.org
1-800-832-2741

Calvert School - *Full Curriculum*
105 Tuscany Road
Baltimore, Maryland 21210
www.calvertschool.org
1-888-487-4652

Sing Spell Read and Write -
Phonics/Reading
International Learning Systems
1000 112th CR N Suite 100
St. Petersburg, FL 33716-9890
1-800-321-TEACH

Oriental Trading Company - *Supplies*
P O Box 2308
Omaha, NE 68103-0308
http://www.oriental.com
1-800-228-2269

The Teaching Home - *Magazine*
P. O. Box 20219
Portland, OR 97294
www.TeachingHome.com
1-503-253-9633

Alpha Omega Publications - *Texts*
300 North McKemy Avenue
Chandler, Az 85226-2618
www.home-schooling.com
1-800-622-3070

Lifetime Books & Gifts
3900 Chalet Suzanne Drive
Lake Wales, FL 33853-7763
http://www.lifetimeonline.com
1-800-377-0390

Bob Jones University Press - *Texts*
Greenville, SC 29614-0062
www.bju.edu
1-800-845-5731

Rod and Staff Publishers - *Texts*
P. O. Box 3 Hwy 172
Crockett, Kentucky 41413-0003
606-522-4348

RLC Company - *Grammar Key*
P O Box 33230
Tulsa, OK 74153
1-800-480-0539

Home School Legal Defense Assoc.
P. O. Box 3000
Purcellville, VA 20134
www.hslda.org
540-338-5600

The Elijah Company - *Texts*
1053 Eldridge Loop
Crossville, TN 38558
www.elijahco.com
1-888-2-elijah

University of Arizona
Extended University - *Gr 1-Univ*
http/www/eu.arizona.edu/corresp
1 -800--772-7480

Sonlight - *Texts* ˏ
8042 South Grant Way
Littleton, CO 80122-2705
www.sonlight-curriculum.com
303-730-6292

A Beka Book, Inc - *Texts*
P. O. Box 19100
Pensacola, FL 32523-9100
www.abeka.org
1-877-223-5226

Tobin's Lab - *Science Eqt.*
P. O. Box 6503
Glendale, Arizona 85312-6503
1-800-522-4776

Glencoe/McGraw-Hill - *Texts*
P O Box 543
Blacklick, OH 43004-0453
1-800-334-7344

Houghton-Mifflin - *Texts*
222 Berkeley Street
Boston, Mass. 02116-3764
1-800-733-2828

Essential Learning Products
Enrichment and Intense Learning
P O Box 2590
Columbus, OH 43216-2590

New Creation Music - *Instruments*
11475 Foxhaven Drive
Chesterland, Ohio 44026
1-800-337-4798
1-216-729-8288

Music Makers Kits - *Kit Instruments*
P O Box 2117
Stillwater, MN 55082-3117
1-612-439-9120

The Music Stand - *Exotic*
Instruments & Rel. Supplies
1 Music Stand Plaza
66 Benning St.
West Lebanon, New Hampshire
1-800-717-7010

Current - *Stationery, Supplies*
The Current Building
Colorado Springs, CO 80941
www.currentcatalog.com
1-800-848-2848

Please be aware that in giving your charge card number over the phone to any individual leaves you open for possible fraudulent or erroneous charges. In the case that you feel that you have been erroneously charged by a supplier, please call your credit card issuer and follow their directions carefully and quickly to preserve your rights under federal laws.

Our family was victim to a type of credit card fraud. Although the resultant difficulties and complications were resolved, it took well over six months to clear our account, even after cancelling the account. Verify exact amounts and name of the person who takes your order. Write down a contact name, the date and time of your order, and keep an itemized list of all items ordered together with pricing, shipping, handling and tax information.

When in doubt, verify availability of product and total price and pay be check. You will, under those circumstances, only place at risk the amount of your check and not additional funds available on your credit line.

This is by no means an endorsement of any of the suppliers listed, but an indication of those available to you. We have ordered from all but a few and have been very satisfied with the results.

Best Wishes to you and your family!